For Fields, Hyder, and Paloma

"The coq de bruyère *is the great fall specialty of La Vallée de la Grande Chartreuse. This magnificent bird flies very high, is very fast on the wing and extremely difficult to shoot. The great trick is to get it at the precise moment when its belly is gorged full of blueberries and raspberries. Then Mademoiselle Ray cleaned out the intestines but left the stomach intact, so that the flavor of the berries permeated the flesh. The birds turned slowly on the spit in front of the roaring, open wood fire. Under each bird was the* lèchefrite *("lickfry"), the metal platter with* le canapé, *the slice of buttered toast catching the drippings from the bird. Finally, the bird was served with* le canapé *as the base on which it rests. The flesh was so juicy and perfumed that no sauce was necessary."*

—Roy Andries de Groot, *The Auberge of the Flowering Hearth*

AFIELD

A Chef's Guide to Preparing and Cooking Wild Game and Fish

Jesse Griffiths   Photographs by Jody Horton

Foreword by Andrew Zimmern

welcome
BOOKS
NEW YORK

Contents

Deer & Turkey

Duck & Goose

Rabbit & Squirrel

The Spring Run

Foreword

Andrew Zimmern

For thousands of years a man was measured in simple terms. Honor and hard work gave him the respect of his peers and status in his community. Over the last century, we have seen that change. Impermanence of lifestyles, class privilege determined solely on wealth, the cultish narcissism of the age of celebrity, and the diminished returns on achievement—these societal woes have all contributed to a cultural standard that our grandparents, who knew that the reward was in the doing, wouldn't recognize. Good or bad, it's a fact. In an age where the world is changing so quickly, in our disposable culture, the ability to pause and put some space between what we think we want and what we decide to do is one of our greatest necessities. Which is why I sought out Jesse Griffiths one day a few years back on a trip to Austin, Texas.

Here was a man living a life that is supremely of the moment, his professional code of conduct couldn't be more fitting with everything that is right about food in America. And more importantly his "way of doing" provides thought leadership and actionable pursuits.

Instinctively we realize that we live in an age where we no longer just want to see recipes with bacon in it, we want to know how to cure the bacon ourselves. So here was a chef who not only was providing us with those answers, he was educating us about lifestyle choices that go beyond the gold standard.

Jesse leads by example. We can talk all we want about sustainability, traditional food arts, great cooking, locally sourced foods, and every other neutered catch phrase of the modern food world, but we need heroes who are willing to show us by doing, not by talking. Jesse is that kind of guy, and trust me they are rare and precious. He is a tireless worker, who hunts and fishes, appreciates our great outdoors, understands the importance of what we need to preserve in our cultural heritage, and translates it for the modern age—is there anything more important? That he chooses to do it in the food space is just the icing on the cake for someone like me.

Nothing is more important, or timely, in the search for a solution to the breakdown to our global systemic food system than the thorough study, reimagining, and ongoing education of Americans on the subject of hunting, fishing, and cooking as an inseparable triptych. If some of our modernist ideas are failing, if production and mechanization compromise our health and well being, if you are curious at all about pursuing solutions instead of tilting at windmills, then you will want to understand fully a food system that is economically, culturally, and environmentally sustainable. Jesse understands at a grassroots level what it takes to live truthfully, in a meaningful way that is deeply felt and personal. He doesn't speak in sound bites or create lifestyle choices with a publicist. He lives and works in accordance with his own principles and that is what I admire about him the most. The benefit we all have is that we can learn from inspiring leaders like Jesse, and act locally while thinking globally. For me the appeal of his book is that it is approachable and engaging for us all.

For those committed to big ideas, or simply for a way to have more fun in the field and in the kitchen, this is a must read. The outdoors-person's approach to food has worked … *does* work … and will always work, and within its ideology are practical ways that anyone interested in changing their world one delicious plate at a time will want to learn about. Slowing down the food systems we sped up, solving our food-health issues, and preserving the best practices of our lost generations are all attainable by living the hunting-cooking lifestyle.

At the end of the day, this is an inspiring collection of stories from the field, replete with 85 recipes that are as delicious as they are fascinating to page through. Anyone who loves food will enjoy this book. The magic, and why I think *Afield* is a special work, is that it fully portrays a way of living and thinking that allows us to return to a more simple way to be measured and respected. And it does so without lecturing or pandering. It reminds me that by living a more principled life, I can make my world a better place and I can use food and cooking to do it. This book is a beautiful piece of work, and after you read it, and cook from it, please get outside and get dirty with it. Wherever you are, the great outdoors is waiting for you, afield.

Introduction

Jesse Griffiths

I once described hunting to my antihunting mother as the same as planting, growing, and harvesting a carrot, just compressed into a few exciting moments. There is the preparation, the commitment, the anticipation, and the payoff—the sad and final moment when the food comes to hand, dead or soon-to-be. A carrot's journey between seed and plate takes about four months, give or take. The span of time between a stick bobber disappearing into a murky creek and a fat crappie flopping onto the bank, or a mourning dove being hit and spiraling down into mesquite thicket is about ten seconds, give or take.

In hunting and fishing, the moment the animal is brought to hand is not the end, but rather the middle of the story. There is still much more work to be done—scaling, skinning, packaging, braising, frying—and the final result is far more rewarding. A gorgeous just-caught fall pompano, gutted and rubbed with olive oil, or a tray full of fresh sausages are the real reasons we spend time afield.

I grew up fishing with my father and only came to hunting in the last few years, which has doubled the time I spend outdoors and pretty much keeps me helplessly distracted year-round. Under the tutelage of many generous people, I have been able to forge a relationship between fish and game and my passion for cooking. This book is not written from the perspective of an expert hunter or fisherman, but from an obsessed one who spends a lot of time preparing and sharing what he catches. Some of the best times I've ever had were with friends on the bank of a river, drinking a little beer and frying up that evening's batch of redbreast sunfish. Or maybe sautéing a fresh venison liver with some bacon and onions after a long, cold day in the woods, knowing that we will have good, ostensibly organic, free-range, grass-fed meat in our freezer for the rest of the year.

Over the past few generations, we've collectively lost the skills that our ancestors possessed to live off the land. Perhaps this is because the need is no longer there, with the proliferation and ubiquity of mass-produced food. Game meats and fresh fish are truly the healthiest proteins you can get your hands on, and, yes, they do taste different than farmed animals. This is because they've fed on wild grasses or minnows or croton seeds, and reflect the beautiful and austere surroundings from which they were gathered. In many cultures, this is perceived as an advantage—a boon to the lucky eater.

This book means not only to explore the world of direct sourcing—that is, being wholly involved in sustaining oneself—but to enlighten and encourage more responsibility and thrift in preparing, cooking, and sharing food from the wild. Hunting and fishing for your dinner gives you a distinct sense of ownership and connection to your own food sources—as well as the responsibilities that come with that, like stewardship, conservation, and a deep respect for life and death.

I don't remember exactly how this project started. I was easily enamored with Jody's photography, and I love the outdoors. I also work round the clock at my job as a chef and wanted to find a way to incorporate hunting and fishing into my daily life somehow. The solution seemed obvious: instruct people to cook what they hunt and fish for, and include good pictures.

Jody is also a hunter and fisherman, but he favors his camera more. He never really puts it down to cast a rod for more than a couple of minutes, and he did once annoyingly take six shots at some doves, dropping four, before casually resuming his photography while I went to collect and pluck his downed birds.

This book allowed us to spend time with our peers and friends who are as attuned to eating well as we are. They are fellow chefs, guides, writers, architects, ranchers, farmers, nurses, teachers, carpenters, lawyers, and, of course, Tink—who defies categorization. Every anecdote shared in the pages that follow is real. Every animal shot or caught was happily eaten and, be assured that we were having a seriously good time throughout.

These stories take place in the Great State of Texas, specifically the Central Texas Hill Country around Austin, where we are blessed with clear-flowing limestone streams, muddy prairie lakes, and pine forests within a couple of hours drive in any direction. Add a couple more hours to that and you have saltwater bays and surf, semi-arid plains, and impenetrable South Texas thickets, teeming with deer, javelinas and huge boars. It is truly a beautiful and bountiful place, but the information contained in *Afield* is germane to any place game or fish are found. We emphatically encourage experimentation and substitution with these recipes depending on the geography and seasons.

What are seasons, really? When hunting, fishing, farming, or foraging, one is, by default, confined to eating seasonally. Just as there's a right and wrong time of year to grow and pick different types of produce, the same is true for wild fish and game. Ducks arrive (here) en masse in late winter; the crappie spawn when the wildflowers pop in the spring and the sunfish will bed up around the first full moon of May or June. Don't ever shoot a rabbit in the summer, unless you want to see some parasites. These natural parameters present a preordained guide to eating what is available throughout the year. This sequence of beginnings and endings wrapped up in a year provides constant opportunity, in perpetuity.

The recipes, or rather the cooking techniques, in this book are based not only on the availability— legal and literal—of fish and game, but of the things that grow around them. This newfangled ideal, practiced since the dawn of time, not only makes sense, but is inherently frugal, pleasantly self-reliant, and it tastes better. As a regimen, place-oriented eating was the norm for every generation up until that of our great-grandparents. Nowadays, you may commonly hear of this style of eating, or food grown without chemicals

and in the proper season as "organic", as being expensive or elitist compared to "conventional" meats and produce. However, food planted with the seasons, hunted in season, and gathered in season was once simply known as *good food*.

With so much time, effort, and resources spent on acquiring our own game, it seems incumbent upon us to spend some energy honoring the animal when we eat it. The pork added to sausage to increase its fat content should be *good* pork, raised happily outside, just like deer; otherwise it's like diluting a dusty, twenty-year-old bottle of Châteauneuf-du-pape with convenience store swill. That venison from the doe you shot that's going in that sausage is some of the best meat available *anywhere* and deserves good company. Good garlic, good salt, good spices, good pig.

The vegetables and fruit that cosmically appear throughout the seasons should likewise be of high quality. If it were up to me, there would be an opening day for strawberries, too, because they just aren't right until they're ready. Sure, you can stretch it out, buying strawberries whenever you *want* them, but they don't *want* to be eaten until they're red and ripe and sweet and from someplace nearby. A very religious and conservative farmer friend once told me regarding food, "You can't always get what you want, but you get what you need." Mr. Alexander's simple tenet of good eating was remarkably enlightening: our food surrounds us, just don't take too much. I also would have never pegged him for a Stones fan.

Treated in this way, food becomes much, much easier to make, not harder. I promise you that. When you hunt, fish, and harvest or buy your ingredients locally, the decisions have already been made for you. Recipes become methods and concepts instead of rote standards. Your shopping list is literally handed to you by your surroundings. And all that's left for you to do is to decide how you want to heat them up.

Dove & Snipe

DOVE : OPENING DAY

It's hard to equate humidity and heat with hunting, but when you've been waiting for several long months, you'll go after these birds in any weather. Such is the weather in mid-September, which is opening day in South Texas—the first day of a promising fall and winter spent afield.

We have scarcely exited the truck and entered the croton field downslope from a ragged stand of oaks—a perfect dove feeding area—when the whir and whistle of a pair of rising

birds takes us by surprise. As with any wing shot I take and make, I am shocked to see the dove corkscrew into the dust between the knee-high weeds that provide the oily black seeds we would later find in the doves' crops while cleaning the birds.

We walk through wide-open fields in the afternoon, downing an occasional bird, missing many more and, sharing a few volleys of friendly grief for missed shots. Finding the dusky gray-and-tan birds seems a miracle on the open, plowed soil, and we spend a good amount of time looking down, simultaneously searching for our dinner and keeping a keen eye and ear out for rattlesnakes attracted by the

fluttering wings of the dying birds in the brush.

With the first birds in the bag, we proceed along a berm marking the southern end of the plowed field, flushing lots of doves and adding to the growing total. I hit a rare double, neatly dropping two birds as they zoom from left to right ten yards in front of me. Working strategically, pushing birds out of the scraggly pin oaks toward the other hunters for passing shots, we slowly near our fair goal: three birds per person for dinner.

Reaching the end of the field near the tank dam, we make our stand. It's that magical time of afternoon when the brutal sun angles down, casting a vague

purple hue over the rolling scrub prairie and sending the doves on their evening errands of drinking, eating, and roosting. At this point we shift from the walking-and-flushing tactic to the stand-and-let-them-come-to-you technique ubiquitous in dove hunting. Standing behind the berm, below a gap in the trees that evidently acts as an aerial landmark on the way to the watering hole behind us, we fire our 20-gauges with regularity as groups of two, five, and twelve speed past us, behind us, at every conceivable angle. The seemingly impossible collision course between our swinging shots and darting birds actually connects with consistency. As the sun goes down far enough to end safe shooting, or finding the birds once shot, we count the bag.

Twenty-nine birds. Perfect, because there are eight of us eating, including the folks back at Loncito's ranch

house who will be pretty happy about dinner, having graciously started the fire for us in anticipation.

Feathers coat everything and will turn up for months to come, like beach sand in a tent. Plucking the tiny birds—although time-consuming—is the best way to enjoy their tiny bounty. The legs and wings, if cooked just right, can be crunched and savored. It's not dainty.

Coated with olive oil and salt, this first game-bird meal is fantastic, simple food. Roasted sweet potatoes; stewed greens; rice spiked with the tiny fried gizzards, hearts, and livers; beer and wine. Lime pie made from the fruit of a giant Mexican lime tree behind the house. The more complicated dove recipes will come later. For now, it's just about eating the whole bird, hot and slightly charred over smoldering pin oak. I am always amazed that just three or four little doves feels like enough to me.

Plucking Doves

Plucking doves whole may get you a little eye-rolling from other hunters, and I know this from experience. These small birds do not yield a lot, and yield even less when just the breasts are removed, as most hunters tend to do. I like to pluck the doves whole, preserving the legs, which will almost double the amount of meat you take home. It's easy. It also gives you something to do while waiting for the next bird to come along. You can drink beer while you do it. In fact, if you're dove hunting with me at one of my spots, you have *to pluck your doves. It's a rule.*

Tools needed: a pair of small scissors

1 Pluck the bird. Pull out the feathers gently towards the head, taking care not to rip the skin. Use your thumb to rub off any remaining pinfeathers and fluff from the bird.

2 Cut the head off at the base of the neck, cutting below the grain-filled crop. Cut the legs off just below the knee.

3 Hold the bird breast down and cut along one side of the spine from the exposed neck area all the way to the tail. Continue cutting around the vent, making a shallow cut just deep enough to go through the skin, avoiding the entrails.

4 Cut around the vent completely and then back up the other side of the spine to the neck. You have now cut out the entire spine and vent in one piece.

5 Grip the exposed spine from the neck end and
pull upward—this should remove all of the entrails,
gizzard, and liver.

6 Remove the hard, round gizzard.

7 Remove the liver.

8 Remove the heart from the bird and set aside.

9 Clean the gizzard: cut the gizzard in half along its equator, exposing its grit-filled interior.

10 The halved gizzard.

11 Pull the membrane lining the middle of the gizzard with your fingernail and remove the membrane and grit. Repeat with the other half.

12 Wash the bird, heart, liver, and cleaned gizzard under cool, running water. Pat dry and place in separate bags (one for birds, one for giblets). Refrigerate for up to 5 days, or wrap tightly in plastic wrap (or vacuum seal) and freeze.

Simple Grilled Doves

This preparation lets the doves shine. You can prepare pigeons the same way, but cook them longer because of their larger size. A hot fire is important—it will cook the little birds quickly, charring the outside and leaving the breasts slightly pink. Try eating the wings and legs from the small birds—bones and all.

12 to 16 whole doves, quail, or snipe, plucked and gutted

About ¼ cup olive oil

Kosher salt and freshly ground black pepper

Serves 4

1. In a large bowl, toss the doves with enough olive oil to coat. Season very well with salt and pepper and set aside for up to 1 hour at room temperature.

2. Meanwhile, build a very hot fire and let it burn down to white coals, or set a gas grill on high heat. Clean the grill grate well and brush it with olive oil.

3. Grill the doves, breast side down, for about 5 minutes, then flip and grill the opposite sides for another 5 minutes, or until the breasts are still firm but pink at the bone. Remove from heat and let rest for about 5 minutes. Serve with rice and greens.

Rice with Gizzards, Hearts, and Livers

Extract a lot of great game bird flavor from tiny gizzards, hearts, and livers, and stretch it with rice to make a meal. Nuttier, chewier brown rice has more nutritional value, and complements the earthy flavors of the organs and onions used in this recipe.

A handful of bird gizzards, livers, and hearts,
   coarsely chopped

3 tablespoons olive oil or lard

Kosher salt and freshly ground black pepper

2 onions, finely chopped

1 cup brown rice

3 cups Game Bird Stock (page 173),
   chicken stock, or water

Serves 4

1. In a heavy-bottomed pot, heat the olive oil or lard over medium-high heat. Add the gizzards, hearts, and livers and cook until nicely browned, about 5 minutes. Season with salt and pepper.

2. Add the onions and cook, stirring occasionally, until softened, about 10 minutes.

3. Add the rice and cook, stirring occasionally, for another 2 minutes.

4. Add the stock, bring to a boil, then lower the heat to a bare simmer. Cover and cook until the rice is tender, about 40 minutes. Fluff the rice with a fork and serve.

Braised Greens

For braising, use any of the wintertime leafy greens, like collards, kale, mustard greens, or turnip greens. Aim for a nice mix of salty, sweet, and sour with the seasonings, so play with the amount of pork, brown sugar, and vinegar until you get a good mix that works with the stout greens. Braised Greens are perfect with Simple Grilled Doves (page 24) or Smothered Boar Chops (page 112).

4 ounces Salted Wild Boar Belly (page 134), pancetta, or bacon, diced

2 onions, sliced

4 garlic cloves, sliced

2 tablespoons brown sugar

¼ cup apple cider vinegar

12 ounces beer

2 bunches winter greens (collard, kale, mustard greens, or turnip greens), coarsely chopped

Crushed red pepper flakes

Kosher salt and freshly ground black pepper

Serves 4

1. In a large pot over medium heat, cook the diced pork, stirring occasionally, until it has rendered some fat and is starting to brown, about 10 minutes.

2. Add the onions and garlic and cook, stirring occasionally, until the onions are tender and fragrant, about 10 minutes.

3. Add the brown sugar and cook for another minute, then add the vinegar, beer, and greens. Bring to a boil, lower the heat, and simmer until the greens are very tender, adding water if necessary, about 45 minutes. Season with red pepper flakes, salt, and black pepper.

Stuffed Doves

These doves—roasted with bacon and stuffed with bread, sage, caraway seed, and lemon—are simple but impressive. Serve them with a fresh, crisp salad and some glazed carrots.

4 tablespoons unsalted butter, melted

2 slices bread, finely diced

1 egg, beaten

2 teaspoons dried sage

1 garlic clove, chopped

1 teaspoon caraway seed

2 tablespoons milk

Zest of 1 lemon

Kosher salt and freshly ground black pepper

8 whole doves, quail, or snipe, plucked
   and gutted

2 tablespoons olive oil

8 slices high-quality bacon

Serves 4

1. Preheat the oven to 400°F.

2. In a medium bowl, combine the melted butter, bread, egg, sage, garlic, caraway, milk, and lemon zest. Season with salt and pepper. Mix well and let sit for a few minutes.

3. Rub each bird with olive oil and season with salt and pepper. Stuff each bird with as much stuffing as it will hold, then wrap a slice of bacon around each breast, tucking the bacon under the wings so that the wings are exposed to more heat and will crisp nicely.

4. Place the birds in a single layer in an ovenproof dish or cast-iron pan. Roast on the top rack of the oven until the bacon is cooked and the birds are firm but still pink on the inside, 15 to 20 minutes. Let the birds rest for a couple minutes before serving.

Bad-Day Dove Risotto

Success afield is never a given, so you learn to work with what you've got. Even one dove can feed two people with this recipe; use it to stretch a day's hunt where the birds were flying with a stiff wind or your barrel was a little bit bent. You can also substitute a cottontail, a teal, or a squirrel for the doves.

1 to 4 whole doves, quail, or snipe, plucked and gutted, with gizzards, hearts, and livers

1 bay leaf

1 tablespoon olive oil

2 slices high-quality bacon, diced

1 onion, finely chopped

2 cups thinly sliced mushrooms (optional)

Kosher salt and freshly ground black pepper

1 cup arborio rice, or try carnaroli or vialone nano

¼ cup white wine

2 tablespoons unsalted butter

¼ cup grated Parmesan cheese

Zest of 1 lemon

Serves 2

1. In a pot over high heat, add the doves (reserving the gizzards, hearts, and livers), bay leaf, and 2 quarts of cold water. Bring just to a boil, lower the heat, and simmer until tender, about 2 hours.

2. Remove the doves and strain the stock into another pot over medium heat to keep it hot.

3. When the doves are cool enough to handle, shred the meat and set aside.

4. Heat olive oil in another pot over medium-high heat. Cook the bacon until it begins to crisp, about 5 minutes. Add the gizzards, hearts, and livers and cook for about 1 minute, stirring often. Add the onion and mushrooms and season with salt and pepper. Cook, stirring often, about 5 minutes more.

5. Add the rice to the pot and cook for a couple minutes more, stirring and stirring, and letting the rice become slightly toasted and fragrant. Add the wine, stirring and scraping the pan well, and cook until the liquid has almost evaporated, about 2 minutes.

6. Add a large ladle of the reserved hot stock to the pot and cook, stirring, until the liquid is absorbed. Continue to add stock to the rice, a little bit at a time, waiting until it is absorbed before adding more, and until the rice is tender but not mushy, 20 to 25 minutes total. The rice should have a little bite left to it, and should be very saucy and slightly pourable, not dense. Adjust as necessary with additional stock; you may not need all of it.

7. Stir in the butter, cheese, lemon zest, and reserved dove meat, and adjust the seasoning with salt and pepper. Serve immediately on warm plates.

Snipe : A Good Day on the Marsh

Eliot is ready to go when Jack and I pull up to his house in the middle of the rice prairie. Hunting snipe, or any game, with Eliot is always a pleasure. He is the Last Gentleman Hunter, a man with a wood-paneled sitting room—adorned with taxidermied whitetail bucks and snow geese, and leather-bound books—where we will sip very nice cognac from tiny crystal cups after dinner. I've only ever seen Eliot in camouflage or black tie, and his dogs are very polite.

These little rockets called snipe are probably the most delicious birds I have ever had. They are delicate—even sweet—and tiny. They make for fast shooting and, invariably, a serious workout walking through knee-high uncut rice.

Today was to be different from the last snipe hunt I went on with Jack, who is Eliot's son-in-law; it was almost a year ago to the day that we embarked on an epic trek, slogging through foot-deep mud for hours, as myriad birdlife swarmed, cackled, and buzzed overhead—geese, ibis, cranes, ducks—only to bag one single snipe. They had flushed wild from their muddy coverts that day and afforded us few shots. Luckily, Eliot pulled through with a few quail from his own afternoon hunt elsewhere, so dinner was had.

Parking at the first likely spot—another uncut rice field—we survey the area and reconnoiter, until a snipe bursts upward with its distinctive *thrippp!*, then banks to one side at eye level, and zooms upward out of range. I've always said that snipe sound like a pencil being dragged loudly against corduroy, but no one has ever seconded that description.

The first field proves to hold no more birds, but

the next one shows promise when Eliot flushes another bird just thirty feet from the truck.

"Hunt here," says Eliot. So we load our guns, take long drinks of water, and empty boxes of number 8s into our shell bags. Little birds need little pellets, and lots of them. My 20-gauge is a short-barreled, heavy, obscure little gun made in Brazil. It shoots a wide pattern and swings well on quick shots.

We walk abreast through the rice, taking laborious steps through mud and waist-high stalks, all the while waiting for that shrill flutter to break the windy drone of the prairie. I flush the first bird and drop it efficiently before it gets a couple of feet above the vegetation. I'm congratulated by Eliot, and gentle Zorro, the black lab, finds the bird after a long search under the matted rice.

Snipe continue to rise occasionally and erratically, and we down a couple and a miss a few. We mark where the escapees come to rest along dikes and canals, and walk in a determined line toward the renewed targets. A map of our progress through the field would appear drunken and frenetic, with the three of us wheeling around at 90-degree angles to track down one bird after another. The monotony of the rice field makes finding birds tough, but the bag is slowly filling, and so far we have four birds in hand.

Soon we cross a dike into new terrain—freshly cut rice—and everyone stops, silently sensing the dramatic change in luck we are about to have. There are snipe everywhere. We can see them scurrying along the muddy tractor-tire ruts from the harvest. Soon they are flushing in ones, twos, and threes, and we are all shooting. Finding the three birds I have downed in the first thirty seconds seems easy compared to our earlier

tribulations in the tall, uncut rice. We turn sharply to the right, walking side by side about twenty yards apart and flushing birds with regularity. This goes on for an hour, culminating in a corner of the field so loaded with snipe that it borders on chaos.

The snipe, by now, are onto us, and have wised up, flying farther out of range and staying low, below the horizon, where they are nigh on invisible in the fading light. We end the day with a dozen beautiful long-beaked birds. A great hunt. I have seven, plus one lost bird that seemed to dissolve into the prairie even after I marked precisely where it had fallen and searched exhaustively.

Tired, we head back to the house for Eliot's oyster stew and biscuits, some good conversation, and an early night. Tomorrow, we're going after some ducks.

Roasted Snipe

This method of skewering—with the birds' own bills—is visually striking and somehow rewarding. Snipe are very, very good eating and should be savored and honored with good wine and good company. Eat them with your hands.

12 whole snipe, plucked and gutted

Several tablespoons olive oil, for brushing

Kosher salt and freshly ground black pepper

12 fresh sage leaves

12 slices high-quality bacon

Serves 4

1. Preheat the oven to 400°F.

2. Dry the snipe well with paper towels, brush lightly with olive oil, and season well with salt and pepper. Lay a sage leaf across each breast and wrap tightly with a piece of bacon, going around the breast and under the wings.

3. Using a wooden or metal skewer, poke a hole through the sides of each snipe right under the rib cage. Remove the skewer and gently insert the snipe's bill all the way through the hole, to hold the bacon in place.

4. Lay the snipe on a baking sheet or roasting pan and roast in the oven for 12 to 15 minutes, or until the bacon begins to crisp and the birds are still slightly pink inside. Let the birds rest for a couple of minutes before serving. Serve with Potatoes Anna (recipe below).

Potatoes Anna

This is proudly adapted from Julia Child's Mastering the Art of French Cooking. *Make the potatoes and have them ready as the snipe emerge from the oven, and then rest the birds directly on top of the crisp, buttery potatoes so that the birdy, bacon-infused juices are absorbed. This side dish is also great with Grilled Venison Loin (page 175), Flounder with Chard and Raisins (page 86), Roasted Duck with Tangerines (page 210) and Confit (page 220).*

1½ pounds potatoes such as Yukon gold or
    Kennebec, peeled

4 tablespoons unsalted butter, melted

Kosher salt

2 tablespoons chopped fresh chives

Serves 4

1. Preheat the oven to 400°F.

2. Slice the potatoes thinly (use a mandoline if you have one) and place in a bowl of cold water. Drain well and put them in a bowl.

3. Heat the butter in a cast-iron pan—a 6-inch pan is perfect—and then pour it over the potatoes, leaving 1 teaspoon in the pan.

4. Season the potatoes with salt.

5. Layer the potatoes in a spiral pattern in the pan—the bottom layer will be the top once inverted. Place the pan in the oven and bake for 40 minutes, or until the potatoes are tender when tested with a thin-bladed knife.

6. Remove from the oven and allow to rest for a few minutes, then carefully invert onto a serving dish. Perch the roasted snipe on top of the potatoes and garnish with the chopped chives.

Hot Fried Birds

Think hot wings, but made with whole birds. The buttermilk marinade tenderizes, but the salacious glaze of butter, honey, garlic, and hot sauce make these really easy to eat. When fried at a high temperature, you get really crisp leg, rib, and wing bones, which can all be crunched and eaten.

12 whole snipe, doves, or quail, plucked and gutted

1 cup buttermilk

Kosher salt and freshly ground black pepper

2 cups all-purpose flour

Lard or oil, for frying

3 tablespoons unsalted butter

4 tablespoons honey

4 garlic cloves, finely chopped

2 or 3 tablespoons hot sauce

4 jalapeño peppers, finely sliced

¼ cup fresh herb leaves, such as fresh parsley or marjoram

Serves 4

1. Cut the birds in half: cut down one side of the breastbone and through the ribs with a sharp, heavy knife. Repeat on the opposite side, effectively removing the breastbone from the birds.

2. Soak the birds in buttermilk for 4 to 12 hours in the refrigerator.

3. Remove from the buttermilk, season well with salt and pepper, and dredge in the flour. Shake off the excess flour and refrigerate the birds for at least half an hour.

4. Heat 4 inches of oil in a fryer or large pot to 375°F.

5. Melt the butter in a small saucepan. Mix the melted butter, honey, garlic, and hot sauce in a large bowl.

6. Fry the birds in batches in the hot oil until golden brown and crisp, 3 or 4 minutes. Drain well on paper towels, brown paper bags, or a rack.

7. Toss the fried birds with the melted-butter mixture, add the jalapeños and herbs, and transfer to a plate. Serve immediately with cold beer.

Creek Fishing

HUNTING FISH

Watching big catfish languidly taking my bait in a clear stream for the first time sealed the deal on my love of sight fishing. I had just moved to Central Texas from North Texas— which is, topographically, culturally, and geographically, quite a distance—and was pretty much spending all of my free time looking for places to fish. Naturally, an area with lots of rivers, and creeks feeding into them, provided me with plenty of opportunity.

The spot I liked best was very close to the downtown area of a quaint tourist trap in the Hill Country. A clear creek ran between massive walls of huge cypress trees draped in Spanish moss, and there was legal access, more or less, to one side. The first time I discovered it, a cursory trip downstream revealed that it was full of fish. Moving slowly so as not to spook them in the clear, shallow water, I spotted sunfish, a few foot-long bass, and even a few catfish, some pushing four or five pounds. Native Rio Grande cichlids, a beautiful, gray-green sunfishlike species with a bulging forehead, were scattered around the calmer eddies and deeper water. This became my go-to spot for years, and I still fish there at least once or twice every season, just to see those trees.

During those trips I was able to hone my skills for fishing small creeks. Many people dismiss bluegills and other sunfish as being gullible and easy, but in the clear water, a very precise presentation was always necessary or they just wouldn't bite. The same went for the catfish, and the bass were almost impossible. I'd be lucky to come home with six fat redbreast sunfish or a couple of medium catfish.

I am recalling this creek as I walk down to another stream not that far from there, thinking about the most important lessons learned from fishing small waterways: namely, how to walk down steep banks and traverse tangled forests of limbs.

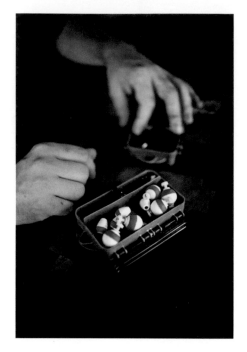

It seems that every creek I fish has a minimum grade of 45 degrees; sometimes it's just a straight drop down to the water. The banks are crowded with lure-snatching brush, and the trees behind you forbid any kind of backcast. You have to walk in a diagonal back and forth just to get to a spot to cast.

Where I am standing today is a good spot. I know that an underground spring enters the stream about twenty feet to my left, forming an oxygen-rich hole, just deep enough that I neither see the bottom nor can tell if there are any fish in there. A bed of weeds along the far bank, thirty feet away, provides more cover for fish, and the channel flows into another deep hole to my right. Walking in, I am aware of my shadow, which is long and extends uncontrollably over the water, so I choose to fish upstream from where I'm standing, as my shadow has no doubt spooked anything down-stream. This creek should produce at any time of year, especially in the late afternoon, when the water is the warmest and the fish will be active and feeding before the steep temperature drop as the sun goes down. This water holds the standard Hill Country mix: largemouth bass, redbreast sunfish, channel catfish, a rare bluegill, and an occasional monster redear sunfish. I caught a dinner-plate-size redear a few hundred yards up from here two years ago.

I cast a tiny black jig out, let it sink to the bottom, and begin a slow, twitching retrieve. This is my go-to lure in this situation, as it's small and mimics most of what the fish might want to eat—aquatic nymphs and the scary-looking hellgrammites. I also love to use live mealworms on these creeks because the fish attack them with forceful prejudice, and even big catfish can't resist these inch-long beige grubs, for some reason. To-day, though, I'm traveling light and without live bait, so I'll go through a series of lures and retrieves until I find what they want.

They do not want the little black jig. I see a couple

of nice largemouth, perfect for grilling, and cast to them, using a faster pace to spur them into striking out of sheer aggression, which likewise fails. I switch to a tiny plastic crawfish and crimp a similarly small split-shot weight about ten inches above. I cast out and drag slowly along the bottom, mimicking the movements of a delicious crawfish that is exposed and fleeing. On the first cast there's a solid thud and I set into a redbreast, which is immediately apparent because of the planing, circular fight and the orange flash in the water. Three casts later, I have another, followed by another. Then, a more solid fish—a small bass, about fourteen inches long, jumps clear out of the water and fights erratically, as bass always do. I have him on the bank and am well on the way to a good meal.

I change gears, looking specifically for a catfish now. I move upstream a bit and thread a small strip of venison liver onto a small gold hook and attach a tiny float about two feet above, with no weight in between so it drifts convincingly. I wait, scanning for the bluish, swaying outline of a catfish. After a few minutes, I spot one in front of me, heading to my right.

I have learned how to approach the cruising catfish, as they are very easily spooked in clear water. Determine their path, and cast about fifteen feet in front of them and about ten feet beyond, then slowly reel the bait in till it crosses their path. They will smell it—it's what they do. Just don't frighten them with a lot of movement.

The liver lands in the weed bed and I pull it smoothly away with the long rod. The catfish is about ten feet downstream and hasn't turned around yet, which they are inclined to do. These stream cats will cruise in pods of one, two, or three, roaming in a circular course around a large pool, sometimes covering stretches of a hundred feet or more. Often, they choose to turn just before they get to your bait, and you wait for them to come by again on their next pass.

This fish moves in the direction of the bait, but about four feet to the left. I think I've missed him when he suddenly turns and I know he's going for it. He's smelled the venison. I see the pale flash of his mouth opening and I think for a moment about how we both like venison liver, when my float steadily goes under and moves downstream at a good clip. I wait until I'm certain that he has the liver in his mouth and firmly set the hook. He responds immediately with the twisting, unpredictable fight of a big creek catfish. I'm using four-pound test line due to the clear water, and have to be extremely careful throughout the whole fight. He fights at first in the open water, but then wises up and zooms toward me and the sunken brush near the bank I'm standing on. I'm saying "no no no" out loud,

trying to urge him back into the open water. I have to tire him fully before I can net him, or he'll break the line. Finally, he gives up and his head is out of the water, exhausted. I slide the net under him and I take the first full breath I've had in five minutes. These creeks are so low profile that they're hardly fished, making them not only very productive, but a pleasant, uncrowded place to be in general. Standing in this same spot, I see squirrels, and watch a committed wood duck hen try to land in the pool at my feet. (I actually turn around, looking for the shotgun that's back at the house) In the summer, there's an occasional snake, incredible mayfly hatches, and fireflies. One morning, hearing a noise behind me, I turned to see a beautiful eight-point buck

staring at me from fifteen feet away. He proceeded to walk away, completely unconcerned. Having these spots is important—they're always good for a small stringer of fish, though you'll never really clean house, nor do you want to. A plateful of fillets or a few whole sunfish, scaled and gutted, are plenty, and these small waters are always full.

I'll cook sunfish and bass (bass are actually technically in the sunfish family, along with crappie, while white bass are true bass) the same way, either frying the fillets (or the whole fish), or baking them with a little butter. The creek version of fish soup (page 76) can also be very good, though it will have its own freshwater character.

Whole Grilled Fish

We often use this preparation for largemouth bass, bluegills, redears, and redbreasted sunfish, but it works well with almost any fish, freshwater or saltwater. Even oily fish like mackerel—especially fish like mackerel—love to be grilled whole over a hot fire. A gas grill is good—but nothing beats a wood fire built of pecan, peach, or oak.

2 medium-size fish or several panfish, about 3 pounds total, whole, gutted, and scaled

Olive oil, for brushing

Kosher salt

1 lemon, halved

Herb Mayonnaise

¾ cup Mayonnaise (page 54) **or Aïoli** (page 76)

¼ cup chopped fresh cilantro, basil, chives, tarragon, dill, or mint, or a combination

Serves 4

1. Make a hot fire in a charcoal grill, or set a gas grill on high heat. Take care that the grill grate is clean.

2. Dry the fish very well with paper towels and brush them all over with olive oil. Season well with salt, including the cavity.

3. Brush the grate with olive oil. Lay the whole fish on the hottest part of the grill and cook, without moving the fish at all, for about 8 minutes; 6 minutes for smaller panfish.

4. Gingerly lift up the fish with a wide, metal spatula and see if it is nicely browned, even a little charred in spots. If so, gently flip the fish and cook on the other side for about 8 minutes. If not, let the fish cook for another 2 to 3 minutes and check again.

5. Once the meat near the head at the thickest part of the shoulders flakes easily and is cooked through, transfer the fish from the grill to a platter.

6. Mix together the mayonnaise and herbs in a small bowl.

7. Squeeze the lemon over the fish and serve immediately with the herb mayonnaise on the side.

Making Mayonnaise

A fine homemade mayonnaise is a thing of beauty, and plays really nicely with fish and game. Mayonnaise is an emulsion of eggs and oil, and can be achieved quickly and with wholesome ingredients if you make your own. Start with great eggs from healthy chickens (there is a risk with eating raw eggs), preferably ones that have foraged on plenty of grass and vegetable scraps. Add horseradish, chopped fresh herbs, chopped pickles, capers, or onion to mayonnaise for a little variation.

1
2
3

Tools needed: a bowl, a whisk, and a cup with a pour spout

1 egg, plus 1 egg yolk, from reputable chickens

1 cup olive oil

1 cup neutral oil, such as safflower, canola or grape seed

Juice of 1 lemon

Salt

Makes 2 cups

1. Place a towel under a steep-sided bowl to keep it in place. Whisk together the egg and the egg yolk until combined. In a cup with a pour spout, combine the olive and neutral oil. Very slowly—a drop at a time—add the oil, whisking all the while.

2. Once the mixture starts to thicken, you may pour the oil in a very small, steady stream, about half the diameter of a pencil, whisking all the while, until all of the oil is incorporated.

3. Squeeze the lemon juice into the mayonnaise and whisk to combine. Season with salt. Add water, if needed, to give the mayonnaise a creamy, not-too-stiff consistency. Add chopped herbs or other garnish. Serve immediately, or refrigerate for up to 2 days.

Cleaning Catfish

The leathery skin of a catfish demands a different approach to cleaning. By first skinning the catfish, you can then either fillet it easily or leave it whole—but gutted—for frying that way, which is a stellar preparation for creek cats in the 14- to 16-inch range. Use the Cornmeal Dredge (page 61) for this, and serve with coleslaw, beans, and beer. Whole smaller catfish can be smoked (page 56).

Tools needed: a sharp fillet knife and a pair of pliers, or a catfish skinner, if you've got one

1. Cut completely around the catfish's head behind the gills with a sharp fillet knife. Make a shallow cut from the gills to the anus and remove the entrails.

2. Peel some of the skin back at the top of the head and grip very firmly with pliers.

3. Grip the catfish's head, minding the sharp spines, and peel the skin off by pulling forcefully towards the tail. Sometimes this is easy, sometimes not. Such is life.

4. Remove the catfish's head by twisting, and then cutting through the spine.

Smoked Catfish Terrine

I spend a lot of time defending catfish, and often quote Willard Scott—the weatherman—for help: "If I go down in for anything in history, I would like to be known as the person who convinced the American people that catfish is one of the finest-eating fishes in the world." Widely believed to be bottom-feeders, many catfish are actually predators that will mostly eat live fish, crustaceans, and maybe a duckling or two. This is true of the ugliest—the yellow, or flathead, catfish—and this is the one you should really seek. A flathead from deep, clear water is an incredibly delicious fish, though its cousins, the channel and blue, can be almost as good if caught from flowing water. Smoking the catfish yields a buttery effect that, when coupled with good cream cheese, makes for a spreadable terrine that is really good with crackers, or made into a sandwich.

2 tablespoons kosher salt

2 tablespoons brown sugar

12 ounces catfish fillets

8 ounces Neufchâtel or cream cheese

2 tablespoons chopped fresh dill or parsley

Zest of 1 lemon

Pinch of ground nutmeg

1 small radish, chopped

A few slices of radish and sprigs of dill (optional)

Serves 4

1. In a small bowl, mix together the salt and sugar. Coat the catfish with this mixture and refrigerate in a plastic bag for about 5 hours.

2. Rinse the fillets and pat dry with paper towel. Then dry, uncovered, overnight in the refrigerator.

3. Preheat a smoker to 225°F with pecan or oak chunks. Hot-smoke the fillets until the fish flakes easily and is cooked through, 20 to 30 minutes.

4. Cool the fillets completely in the refrigerator, then coarsely shred the fish into a bowl. Mix in the cream cheese, chopped herbs, lemon zest, nutmeg, and radish.

5. Line a ramekin or small bowl with plastic wrap. Lay a few slices of radish and sprigs of dill on the bottom for presentation. Fill with the catfish-and-cream-cheese mixture. Chill for about 1 hour, then unmold onto a plate and serve with grilled bread or crackers.

Frying Fish

Frying is arguably the best way to have fish, or a lot of different foods, actually. Below are three different methods of frying fresh fish: in a batter, in a traditional cornmeal coating, and using a batter–bread crumb hybrid of sorts. All rely on the same tenets to make the recipe a success: hot oil, cold fish, and cold batter. Don't crowd the fryer and do drain the finished fried fish very well on absorbent paper or a rack. We like peanut oil for frying, but nonhydrogenated lard is also superb, though expensive if you don't have access to such things. Using a temperature-regulated deep fryer can make the process much easier, but don't be afraid to attempt frying fish without one—just be patient and organized. Eat fried fish immediately, with beer, coleslaw, and cold pickles.

Beer Batter

Obviously, the beer will influence the outcome of the batter. Experiment with different beers—dark beers can be excellent in this application.

1½ **pounds medium or small fish fillets**

Kosher salt

12 ounces cold beer

1 cup all-purpose flour

Lard or oil, for frying

Serves 4

1. Season the fillets with salt.

2. Mix the beer and flour until just blended, then refrigerate until cold.

3. Heat 4 inches of oil in a fryer or large pot to 375°F. When the oil is hot, dip the fish in the batter, let the excess drip off, and carefully lower the fish into the oil. Fry in batches until golden, 3 to 5 minutes, depending on the size of the fillet.

4. Carefully remove the fish with a skimmer, or by raising the fry basket, and gently rest the fillets on paper towels, brown paper bags, or a rack.

5. Sprinkle the fillets with salt. Serve immediately with malt vinegar, tartar sauce, aïoli, high-quality ketchup, or cocktail sauce.

Mustard Batter

This is the hybrid—a thin batter that is rolled in bread crumbs. This batter works well with stronger-flavored fish like white bass or catfish, but is also good with most any fish. Again, using different mustards (whole grain, Dijon, yellow) and different beers will affect the outcome in good ways. In camp or in a rental fish shack in a small town, just use what you've got.

1½ pounds medium or small fish fillets

Kosher salt

12 ounces cold beer

1 egg

2½ cups all-purpose flour

½ cup mustard

3 cups unseasoned bread crumbs

Lard or oil, for frying

Serves 4

1. Season the fillets with salt.

2. In a medium bowl, mix the beer, egg, ½ cup of the flour, and the mustard, then refrigerate until cold.

3. Dredge the fillets first in the remaining flour, then in the mustard batter, and then in the bread crumbs. Make sure the fillets are evenly coated with the bread crumbs. Refrigerate for up to 2 hours, until ready to fry.

4. Heat 4 inches of oil in a fryer or large pot to 375°F. When the oil is hot, carefully lower the fish into it. Fry until golden, 3 to 5 minutes, depending on the size of the fillet.

5. Carefully remove the fish with a skimmer, or by raising the fry basket, and gently rest the fillets on paper towels, brown paper bags, or a rack. Serve immediately with your preferred condiments.

Cornmeal Dredge

The classic dredge. Using extra finely ground cornmeal gives a superior crunch to this preparation. Serve this with beans and coleslaw.

1½ pounds medium or small fish fillets

Kosher salt and freshly ground black pepper

2 eggs, beaten

1 cup milk

2 cups finely ground cornmeal

Lard or oil, for frying

Serves 4

1. Season the fillets with salt and pepper.

2. Mix together the eggs and milk. Dip the fillets first into cornmeal, then into the egg mixture, then back into the cornmeal. Shake off the excess and refrigerate until cold.

3. Heat 4 inches of oil in a fryer or large pot to 375°F. When the oil is hot, carefully lower the fish into it. Fry in batches until golden, 3 to 5 minutes, depending on the size of the fillet.

4. Carefully remove the fish with a skimmer, or by raising the fry basket, and gently rest the fillets on paper towels, brown paper bags, or a rack. Serve immediately.

Coleslaw

I like coleslaw simple, crisp, and vinegary. With rich fried fish or smoked meats—which coleslaw usually accompanies—an acidic foil is needed for balance. Vary the amount of sugar to suit your tastes, but do use a lot of black pepper.

1 medium head of cabbage, about 1 pound

½ cup apple cider vinegar

2 tablespoons whole-grain mustard

Kosher salt and freshly ground black pepper

1 tablespoon sugar

1 teaspoon celery seed

Serves 4

1. Core the cabbage and slice as thinly as you possibly can.

2. Toss the cabbage in a large bowl with the vinegar, mustard, salt, plenty of black pepper, sugar, and celery seed.

3. Refrigerate for at least 1 hour, and up to 2 days.

4. Serve cold with fried fish or grilled meats.

tide, and the inherent deliciousness of the things that live there. In fact, I do not have one fish on, but rather two. A fat but smallish whiting is attached to each hook. An instant double is just what you want when you're hungry and it's almost dark.

Jody builds a very nice, intensely hot fire as per my request. I rebait, lose a couple of pieces of squid to fish, miss a couple of strikes, and land another small whiting. Then I get another solid strike, a good fish for sure, but it's gone immediately. Also gone is the hook, and a good portion of the heavy monofilament line, indicating that something sizeable and sharp toothed is in the area. I judge this as the right time to get out and cook the whiting, remembering the story that a pilot told me of his frequent flights over this stretch of coastline. It seems that from the air you can see the silhouettes of sharks in the surf. He swore he would never get in the water down here.

I gut and scale my whiting and rinse them in the crashing waves, reminding myself to clean my pocket-knife well when we get back to the house so it won't rust. The fire is perfect and the fish get a quick rub of olive oil and a sprinkling of salt, which I have to start a couple of feet upwind in the stiff breeze coming inland. The fish cook quickly, and go perfectly with the hot, sour carrot-top sauce and a really cold beer.

Whole Grilled Whiting with Carrot-Top Sauce

This is an excellent use for lacy green carrot tops, which have a great fresh parsley flavor with a hint of sweet carrot. Use only very fresh carrot tops from good carrots, or substitute parsley. Other small or medium-size fish from the surf or bay can be substituted—try croaker, redfish, sand trout, or speckled trout. The carrot-top sauce is also very good on grilled meats like venison.

8 small or 4 large whiting, whole, gutted and scaled

Olive oil, for brushing

Kosher salt and freshly ground black pepper

Lemon wedges

Carrot-Top Sauce

1 cup finely chopped carrot-top greens

¾ cups olive oil

½ cup red wine vinegar

2 tablespoons sugar

5 garlic cloves, minced

1 tablespoon dried oregano

Kosher salt and freshly ground black pepper

1 teaspoon or more crushed red pepper flakes

Serves 4

1. Whisk together all of the ingredients for the carrot-top sauce. Taste and adjust the salt, pepper, and red pepper flakes. Set aside.

2. Dry the fish very well with paper towels and brush all over with olive oil. Season well with salt, including the cavity.

3. Make a hot fire in a charcoal grill, or turn a gas grill up to high heat. Clean the grill grate well and brush it with olive oil.

4. Lay the whole fish on the hottest part of the grill and cook, without moving the fish, until browned and crisp, about 4 minutes.

5. Gently flip the fish and cook on the opposite side until browned and crisp, about 4 minutes.

6. Finish the fish by grilling for 1 minute more on its belly.

7. Carefully transfer the fish to a platter, spoon on the carrot-top sauce, and serve with lemon wedges.

The Half-Shell Technique

Cutting fish in this manner is very popular, as it's generally easier and yields a fillet that lends itself to cooking simply while retaining a lot of its moisture. This technique is commonly used for tough-skinned fish such as black and red drum, which can dull a fillet knife in seconds with their armorlike scales.

The fish is roughly filleted, going straight down the backbone and leaving the skin, scales, and rib bones attached. The fillet is then grilled over a hot fire, skin and scale sides down. The flesh is insulated by the thick scales while cooking.

Tools needed: a sharp fillet knife and a large, heavy knife, longer than the fish's vertical dimension

1. Gut the fish by cutting from the anus to the gills with the fillet knife, and pull out all of the viscera inside the cavity. Rinse the cavity very well. Make a cut right behind the head, angling forward over the fish's eyes to get the meat found here. Angle the knife blade toward the head, coming up under the scales to avoid cutting through them. Cut all the way to the spine from the top of the fish to the belly.

2. Holding the fillet knife horizontally, insert the tip and cut along the top of the fillet from the head to the tail along the backbone.

3. With the heavy, longer knife, cut through the rib bones, peeling the entire fillet from the fish's side. Repeat with the other side. Save the bones for fish stock.

Half-Shell Tacos

This is a traditional coastal preparation that is superquick, easy, and very effective. It applies particularly well to tough-scaled fish like sheepshead, and to drum (red and black). In freshwater, try it with a largemouth bass. Leaving the scales and skin on the fillet and cooking it over high heat not only imparts a great smoky, charred flavor, but insulates the fillet as it cooks, leaving it very tender and infused with the seasonings you choose. Here, we opt for Mexican oregano, lime, and hot paprika. Tacos are a perfect dinner after a day of fishing when you're hungry and need something quick to go with the beers.

2 large fish fillets, skin and scales on, about 1 pound each (page 69)

Kosher salt and freshly ground black pepper

1 tablespoon dried Mexican oregano

1 teaspoon hot paprika

4 tablespoons unsalted butter, softened

3 limes, thinly sliced

12 corn tortillas

¼ head green cabbage, chopped

2 avocados, diced

A few sprigs of cilantro

Vinegary hot sauce

Serves 4

1. Make a hot fire in a charcoal grill, or set a gas grill on high heat.

2. Season the fish with salt and pepper.

3. In a small bowl, mix together the oregano, paprika, and butter. Spread the butter mixture evenly over the fillets, then layer the sliced limes on top.

4. Grill the fillets, skin side down, covered, for 12 to 20 minutes, depending on thickness, until the fish flakes easily and is cooked through.

5. Remove the fillets. Pull the cooked fish from the skin with a large spoon, discarding the skin and any bones.

6. Quickly heat the tortillas on the grill. Make tacos with the warmed tortillas, fish, cabbage, avocado, cilantro, and hot sauce.

Fish and Oyster Stew with Salted Wild Boar Belly

This is a variation on the most unlikely of delicious soups: the milk-based oyster stew of the South. Basically just oysters poached in milk and seasoned with pepper, the dish relies heavily on the garnish: crisp toast and the vinegar-based hot sauce that magically adds acidity and life. Pork naturally complements seafood, and earthy salted wild boar belly marries well with the saline oysters in this dish.

8 ounces Salted Wild Boar Belly (page 134) or salt pork, diced

½ teaspoon dried oregano

½ teaspoon dried thyme

1 bay leaf

2 quarts milk

1 pint shucked oysters in their liquor

2 large mild whitefish fillets, such as drum, redfish, snapper, flounder, or grouper, about 1 pound, cut into large pieces

Kosher salt and freshly ground black pepper

4 slices good bread

2 tablespoons unsalted butter

Vinegary hot sauce

Serves 4

1. In a large pot over medium heat, brown and crisp the pork belly, about 10 minutes.

2. Add the dried herbs and bay leaf to the pot and continue to cook for about 20 seconds more, or until fragrant.

3. Add the milk and bring to a simmer.

4. Add the oysters with their liquor, and the fish, then turn off the heat. Let the fish and oysters slowly poach until done, about 5 minutes; the oysters will curl at the edges when ready. Season with salt and plenty of pepper.

5. Toast bread slices until nicely browned on each side and butter them.

6. Serve the stew very hot with the buttered toast and hot sauce.

Smoked Mullet Salad with Apples

Mullet has a dense, flaky texture that smokes very well, and you'll have zero competition while fishing the bays for them. They're best caught with cast nets, as they're plant feeders and won't hit lures or bait, but you can also gig them at night. Try for medium-size fish in the 12- to 18-inch range, gut them quickly, and get them on ice.

2 pounds fresh mullet fillets

⅓ cup salt

⅓ cup sugar

5 garlic cloves, sliced

1 teaspoon freshly ground black pepper

½ teaspoon ground ginger

½ teaspoon hot paprika

1 tablespoon plus 1 teaspoon coarse-ground mustard

1 tablespoon honey

1¼ teaspoons kosher salt

½ teaspoon freshly ground black pepper

4 tablespoons olive oil

½ onion, thinly sliced

2 apples, thinly sliced

1 head Bibb or other crisp lettuce

Serves 4

1. Rinse the fillets well and pat dry with paper towels.

2. In a bowl, combine the salt, sugar, garlic, pepper, ginger, and paprika, and coat the fillets evenly. Cure for 12 hours in the refrigerator, then rinse very well and dry, uncovered, on a rack in the refrigerator for 4 hours or up to 1 day.

3. Preheat a smoker and hot-smoke the fillets at 225°F until completely cooked through, about 45 minutes. Cool immediately and wrap well in plastic wrap. The smoked mullet will keep for about 1 week in the refrigerator.

4. In a bowl, whisk together the mustard, honey, salt, and pepper. Slowly add the olive oil, whisking the whole time. Add the onion and let stand for 20 minutes.

5. Roughly shred the meat from the smoked mullet, making sure to remove the fishy, muddy, dark bloodline.

6. Toss the shredded mullet and the apple slices with the onion dressing. Arrange lettuce leaves on four plates, then top with the dressed mullet mixture. Serve immediately.

Arroz Abanda

This is a Valencian Spanish preparation that utilizes fish fillets and bones to make an incredibly savory rice dish that is served with an intense garlic mayonnaise. When done correctly, a slightly charred crust will form on the bottom of the pan, and this should be fought over. The key is watching for the liquid to finally be absorbed by the rice, and then listening for the sizzle of the crust forming after the sounds of bubbling fish stock cease. Use black drum, redfish, snapper, small grouper, croaker, whiting, triggerfish, sheepshead, or speckled trout for this recipe.

4 pounds whole fish, gutted, gilled, and filleted, bones reserved

1 bay leaf

4 sprigs thyme

1 teaspoon fennel seed

½ cup olive oil

4 ripe tomatoes, halved and grated

8 garlic cloves, finely chopped

1 onion, chopped

1 medium red bell pepper, seeded and finely chopped

¾ cup chopped fresh parsley

Pinch of saffron threads

1½ cups short-grain rice (preferably Spanish bomba, but can substitute carnaroli or arborio)

¼ cup white wine

Kosher salt

1 recipe Aïoli (page 76)

1 lemon, quartered

Serves 4

1. In a large pot over high heat, combine 1 gallon of water, the fish bones, bay leaf, thyme, and fennel seed. When the stock begins to show small bubbles, lower the heat just enough to maintain a simmer. Simmer for 45 minutes, skimming any foam that rises to the surface. Strain the stock through a fine-mesh strainer into another pot and keep warm.

2. In a large cast-iron or paella pan, heat the olive oil over medium heat. Add the tomatoes, garlic, onion, red bell pepper, ½ cup of the parsley, and saffron. Cook, stirring often, for 10 to 12 minutes, or until thickened, concentrated, and beginning to stick to the bottom of the pan.

3. Add the rice and cook, stirring, for 2 minutes. Add the white wine and salt and cook for 2 minutes more, then add 6 cups of the warm reserved fish stock. Bring to a boil, lower the heat, and simmer until the rice has absorbed the liquid, 30 to 35 minutes, adding more stock if the rice is not cooked through.

4. Once the rice is tender and the liquid is absorbed, allow the rice to cook for a few minutes more, listening for a sizzle as a crust forms on the bottom of the rice. Once it has sizzled for a couple of minutes, remove the pan from the heat.

5. Reheat the remaining fish stock until small bubbles form, then turn off the heat. Add the fillets to the stock and let cook until just done, 3 to 4 minutes for a medium-size fillet.

6. Carefully remove the fillets with a slotted spoon and serve over rice with very generous amounts of aïoli, lemon, and the remaining chopped parsley. Use a thin metal spatula to remove the crusty rice from the pan.

Fish Soup

I learned to love fish soup because I kept catching little whiting while fishing for flounder. I had come a long way to catch some fish, and no way was I leaving without a meal, so soup it was, and it worked. This recipe is now our signature dish.

4 pounds very fresh whole fish: snapper, grouper, redfish, whiting, or flounder

4 bay leaves

¼ cup olive oil

1 onion, sliced

1 red bell pepper, sliced

½ teaspoon cumin seed

½ teaspoon coriander seed

½ teaspoon fennel seed

Kosher salt

2 cups canned tomatoes or fresh chopped tomatoes

½ cup white wine

4 small new potatoes, halved

Juice of 1 lemon

Chopped fresh cilantro, basil, or parsley

1 recipe Aïoli (below)

4 slices grilled or toasted bread

Serves 4

1. Fillet the fish and cut into 1-inch pieces. Reserve the bones.

2. In a large soup pot, add the fish bones and 2 bay leaves to 2 quarts of water and bring to a boil over high heat. Reduce the heat to simmer and cook for 45 minutes, skimming off any foam that rises to the surface.

3. In another large pot, heat the olive oil over medium heat and add the 2 remaining bay leaves, onion, bell pepper, and spices, Season with salt. Cook, stirring occasionally, until the vegetables are softened and fragrant, about 10 minutes. Do not brown.

4. Add the tomatoes to the onion and peppers and cook for another 10 minutes, stirring often.

5. Add the white wine and pour 6 cups of the fish stock through a fine-mesh strainer into the pot. Bring to a simmer. Add the potatoes and simmer until tender, about 15 minutes.

6. Season the soup with salt and lemon juice, remove from the heat and add the fillet pieces. Allow the fish to cook for about 5 minutes, or until the fish flakes easily.

7. Divide the soup among four bowls, garnish with chopped herbs, and top each bowl with a slice of toast spread with aïoli.

Aïoli

12 garlic cloves

Kosher salt

1 egg, plus 1 egg yolk

1 cup olive oil

Makes 1 cup

Mash the garlic with the salt with the side of a heavy knife until it is a thick paste. Add this to the egg and egg yolk and whisk well. Follow the directions in Making Mayonnaise (page 54), whisking the olive oil in slowly until a thick emulsion is formed. Aïoli is traditionally not seasoned with lemon or thinned with water, but you may do as you will.

Flounder & Crab

FLOUNDER : THE BAY AT NIGHT

Our second day on the coast, we are still trying to find a kindly local to take us after some flounder. My saltwater career began in pursuit of flounder with a rod and reel, which can be fun, but is not very productive. The first annual trips to the ocean were always during the windy, cold November run when the flounder empty from the shallow, muddy bays and head toward the deep Gulf to spawn. We would wade all day long, casting live shrimp or the indestructible mud minnows along tiny channels and reedy marsh outflows for flounder that would lie in wait on the sandy seafloor.

Flounder are designed to ambush upward, which is why their eyes are on one side of their head, and they are white on the bottom. They are fish turned on their sides and flattened, and are efficient predators despite their odd design. Their maddening strike, which would come after hours of no bites at all, is a fierce, single tap. This is the flounder opening its large mouth, which houses some serious canine/vampire-style teeth—I know this because I was bitten by a flounder once. The hard part is that after the tap, you have to just wait. You count to ten, slowly, then tighten the line and, if there's still tension, set the hook hard. During this interim, the flounder has been slowly engulfing its prey after stunning it with the initial strike. There are few better feelings than setting the hook after this long, tense pause and actually feeling the fish on the other end.

I think that our best days yielded three or four flounder. Not bad, considering that a flounder has a lot of meat on it, and can feed three or four people if it's in the eighteen-inch range. These were some of my favorite times, and they eventually stopped due to the combined entropy of destructive hurricanes and life.

Now I am back at the coast and we are about to go get flounder the way people who get flounder for a living do it—with a spear. Our queries about someone to take us flounder gigging have not been fruitful, until I get a late-afternoon call from Captain David, who says he can take us out that night. He seems very friendly on the phone and things are looking up.

A squall passes over us as the sun heads down, threatening the whole night's fishing. Standing on an elevated platform of a boat holding a metal pole is not a good idea in a thunderstorm, but Captain David assures us it's passing quickly and to still come down. Jody is leery, but I remind him that dead customers are bad for business, so if Captain David says it's okay, it's okay—and I mostly believe it. We enjoy the rain for a few minutes—there is an historic drought back at home at the time—and head to the docks.

David is easy to spot and ready to go. A flounder-gigging boat looks like a floating rock concert. It's a flat-bottomed, large bay boat with a big engine that resembles a giant leaf blower, and racks of really bright lights around the front and sides. The method is simple: cruise around in very shallow water, look for flounder, and then stab them.

We set out, chatting with the very amiable captain, and head quickly across the bay in complete darkness, trusting this young guide not to hit a crab trap or buoy on the way, which he does not. We pull up along a weedy shoreline, David hits the leaf blower and the stadium lights, and we start a slow cruise in about six inches of water. A whole world of nighttime bay life becomes apparent, and we are a bit captivated. Mullet scoot everywhere, and small crabs, black drum, and sheepshead flit around the weeds and oyster shells, dodging our glowing boat. After about ten minutes,

David, who is standing next to me on the bow platform of the boat staring intently at the aquariumlike bay floor, slows the boat suddenly and dramatically and points right in front of us, about five feet from my toes.

"There!" he announces. There! Wait—where? I see nothing except oyster shells and olive drab clumps of weed. Then I see it—a flounder-shaped outline. I distinguish the head from the tail, line up the four-pronged gig and drive it home, feeling a sandy crunch of metal tines meeting shell and rock, and the definite movement of a big flounder, now pinned against the bay floor. It fights for a moment, and then I sweep the long pole with the heavy flatfish on the end into a cooler right behind me that is equipped with a rudimentary but effective cover that allows one to pull the skewered flounder off the gig. Jody snaps a few shots of the white-bellied fish, which has a beautiful, almost fractal beige pattern on its top side. Chameleonlike, these flounder found hiding above oyster shells have round sunflower-shaped patterns that will fade completely by the time we get them home.

David unabashedly and sincerely pats me on the back, and I can see that this guy really loves what he does, which is a great trait in a guide, and not at all common anymore. He is obviously excited, and leads us to catch both of our limits of flounder—ten fish—in the matter of an hour. I can't help but think, every time I deposit another big slab of flounder in the cooler, that that's dinner for four people. And if you've had flounder before, you know there's even more to it. Texturally and flavor-wise, it is the king of the bay. David has an uncanny ability to spot these obscured fish, and when asked how often his clients are able to see the hidden fish before he does, he just laughs.

Black drum and sheepshead—two other fish that are pretty damn good—are also legal targets for giggers, but we do not see any of legal size. The sight of a small black drum darting into a billowing weed bed reminds me of the last time I was in this same bay fishing for black drum, with my gregarious lamb-ranching buddy Loncito, who seems to know everybody in South Texas, including every fishing guide in the area. After an evening of eating fried soft-shell crabs and drinking wine, Loncito's friend Butch, a local guide, agreed to take us into the back lakes of the bay complex to the north of the island we were staying on. The boat ride was impressive. Butch, a Vietnam vet with a gentle demeanor and understated drawl, took us on a fast run in his bay boat the next morning along a private shoreline, identifying the ducks (he guides for them, too), other birdlife, and landmarks that are part of his daily world. These "back lakes" are channels, narrow and wide, that crisscross the far side of the barrier islands along the coast, and are marshy mazes of shallow water and deep holes, depending on the level of the tide. Many people rightfully avoid these areas because they are so hard to navigate.

Butch swung us wide around a point, then aimed us right for a shallow break in the shoreline of one island. I was sure there was no way we could fit the boat, albeit a boat with a very shallow draft, through the gap, which appeared to have no more than six inches of water in it. As we neared the cut, Butch turned a bit, angling the boat right into the invisible channel that crossed through the bank at a harsh diagonal. Soon we were in a wide, deep channel with scrubby coastal banks on either side, and Butch was scanning the water for schools of black drum. Compared to its flashier and more widely known cousin, the redfish—or red drum—blacks are, in my opinion, a frequently underrated fish. Butch's method is exciting, too: catch the first one and let it fight without bringing it in, a method I first saw when fishing for mahimahi in Costa Rica. The others in the school will stay close, curious about the

ruckus, at which point you hook the next one and bring in the first. Repeat until you've hit your limit.

We didn't hit limits that day or even come close. Butch was disappointed, but Loncito and I didn't care a bit. Two or three black drum and a bonus red were in the bucket and we had a great boat ride.

I see some larger mullet and I ask Captain David about the mostly Florida-based tradition of eating them. He is unimpressed and not really excited about the prospect of eating "trash fish," but readily allows me to gig one fat mullet and put it into his classy flounder box. I have always wondered about these fish. They are everywhere and, as herbivores that school in shallows, easily caught in cast nets as bait. Larger ones are omnipresent in the bay, and I'm curious to know if they're good eating. Evidently, in Florida, they are consumed with abandon, with whole restaurants devoted to smoked mullet.

So what do they know in Florida that we don't? Or is it a different species or sub-species? Is it environmental, with a varied forage base influencing the flavor of the fish?

Back at the dock, a retired flounder gigger is waiting for us, or actually waiting for his buddy David. With the casual friendliness of someone who doesn't work anymore and just fishes, he chats with us on the dock as David tidies the boat and begins unloading the flounder. I notice that he hasn't touched the gigged mullet; finally, he sheepishly transfers it to the dock.

"What the hell is that?" his friend asks.

"He wanted to get it," David says, pointing at me.

"Have you ever tried it?" I ask the retiree.

"Hell no."

Right. We pack our cooler full of gutted and gilled flounder and one mullet, which Captain David does not gut and gill for us, and head to our temporary home. It's just past midnight.

Filleting Flounder **Tools needed:** a sharp, thin-bladed fillet knife.

1 Make a cut from behind the flounder's gills to the tail at a point about halfway up the side of the fish. Do not cut through bones.

2 Using the tip of the knife, follow the bones along the bottom fillet all the way to the fin.

3 Repeat this process, removing the top fillet by following the contour of the bones. Cut above the flounder's head at an angle and remove the fillet.

4 Top fillets are removed.

5 Make a similar cut along the bottom side of the flounder from the gills to the tail, following the backbone.

6 Remove these smaller bottom fillets.

7 Grip the flounder skin at the tail end and cut the fillet away, keeping the knife at a slight angle.

8 Repeat with remaining fillets. Save the bones and skin; flounder makes excellent fish stock.

Baked Flounder with Parsnips and Carrots

This dish plays off of the natural sweetness of flounder, carrots, and parsnips. It is really a dish of its ingredients, so choose the carrots and parsnips well, because they carry the recipe. Serve this dish as its own course, with no sides, possibly preceded by something with different flavors, like a game terrine or something acidic and pickled. Drink a sweet white wine.

4 flounder fillets, about 1½ pounds

Kosher salt

4 medium carrots

4 medium parsnips, peeled

2 tablespoons olive oil

6 tablespoons unsalted butter, softened

**2 teaspoons fresh thyme leaves,
    plus 4 sprigs thyme**

Zest of 1 small lemon

Serves 4

1. Preheat the oven to 375°F.

2. Season the fillets with salt and set aside.

3. Grate the carrots and parsnips into a bowl, then toss well with olive oil and a pinch of salt.

4. In another small bowl, mix together the butter, thyme leaves, and lemon zest and set aside.

5. In a gratin dish or on a baking sheet, lay the grated parsnips and carrots out in four piles the size of the fillets. Lay the fillets on top and spread the seasoned butter on each fillet. Top each fillet with a thyme sprig.

6. Bake the flounder for 20 to 25 minutes, or until the fish easily flakes and is cooked through. Serve immediately.

Sautéed Flounder with Chard and Raisins

Savory brown butter, Swiss chard, lemon, and sugary raisins set off the amazing flavor of fresh flounder, which has enough character to stand up to the salty, bitter, sour, and sweet components of this dish.

4 flounder fillets, about 1½ pounds

Kosher salt and freshly ground black pepper

8 tablespoons (1 stick) unsalted butter

1 cup all-purpose flour

Juice of 1 lemon

¼ cup chopped fresh parsley

1 tablespoon olive oil

2 garlic cloves, thinly sliced

2 large bunches of chard, chopped and
  washed well

½ cup raisins

Serves 4

1. Season the fillets with salt and pepper.

2. In a pan large enough to hold all of the fillets in a single layer, melt the butter over high heat.

3. When the butter is very hot, dredge each fillet in the flour and place in the pan. Cook the fillets until browned on one side, about 3 minutes. Carefully flip the fillets and cook until the fish flakes easily and is browned on the other side, 2 to 3 minutes more.

4. Carefully remove the fillets from the pan and set aside. Turn off the heat, add the lemon juice and parsley to the butter remaining in the pan, stir, and set aside.

5. In another large pan, heat the olive oil over medium-high heat. Add the garlic and cook about 30 seconds, until it just starts to brown. Add the chard, raisins, and ¼ cup water, and cook, stirring, until the chard is wilted and tender, about 3 minutes. Season with salt and pepper.

6. Divide the chard among four plates. Place a fillet on each plate and top with some of the butter-and-lemon sauce. Serve immediately.

Preparing Flounder for Stuffing

1 Holding the spoon or fish scaler perpendicular to the body, scrape the scales from the flounder, tail to head. Make sure to include the areas near the fins, belly, and head.

2 Repeat on the bottom (white area) of the flounder.

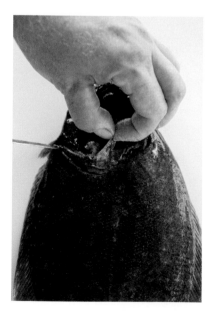

3 Make a cut behind the gills, following the gills to the belly.

4 With the tip of the knife, continue the slit lengthwise along the fish just to the end of the stomach cavity.

Tools needed: a sharp, thin-bladed fillet knife and a spoon or fish scaler

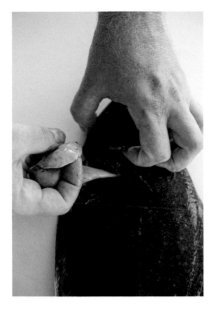

5 Pull back the flap and firmly remove the guts from the cavity.

6 Grasping the fish firmly, make a cut along the backbone, which runs lengthwise along the middle of the (brown) top of the flounder.

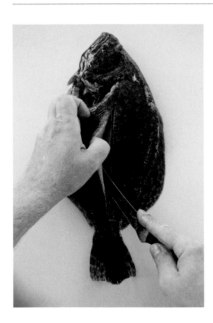

7 To make a pocket for stuffing, insert the tip of the knife horizontally toward the belly side; slide the knife under the flesh to separate it from the rib bones almost to the fins on the belly.

8 Turn the flounder around and make another lengthwise pocket, again sliding the knife along the bones almost to the fins on the other side.

Roasted Whole Flounder with Herbs and Potatoes

This is a simple and effective way of roasting a flounder that not only utilizes the whole fish, but also keeps the delicate flesh moist. Don't miss the cheek meat, the crisp tail, and the soft meat around the flounder's prominent fins. The remaining bones can even be saved for use in a simple fish stock, and the leftover meat can be reheated for tacos.

6 medium potatoes, halved

2 tablespoons olive oil

Kosher salt

4 tablespoons unsalted butter, softened

1 tablespoon each chopped fresh thyme
   and oregano

6 garlic cloves, minced

6 ounces picked blue crabmeat (optional)
   (page 94)

1 large flounder, 2 to 3 pounds, scaled
   and prepared for stuffing (page 88)

3 bay leaves

3 thin slices lemon

¼ cup chopped fresh parsley

Serves 4

1. Preheat the oven to 400°F.

2. In a large roasting pan, toss the potatoes in 1 tablespoon of the olive oil, season with salt, and roast for 25 minutes.

3. Mix together the butter, herbs, garlic, and crabmeat, if using, and spread in the cavity of the fish. Lay the bay leaves on top of the mixture and then the lemon slices. Brush the flounder with the remaining olive oil, then season with salt.

4. Place the flounder in the roasting pan with the potatoes and bake for 20 minutes, or until the flounder is tender and cooked through.

5. Carefully remove the flounder from the pan. If the potatoes are not browned on top, spoon some of the melted butter and pan juices over them and broil for 4 to 5 minutes, or until nicely browned.

6. Sprinkle the flounder and roasted potatoes with the parsley and serve immediately.

Cooking with Fresh Herbs

Fresh herbs are referred to constantly throughout the book because they are very important. The simple act of planting a few herbs in a pot or in a small bed can greatly improve the flavor and vitality of food, and, once established, a small herb garden is almost self-sustaining. Start with some perennial herbs that will grow year-round, like rosemary, oregano, and thyme. These need some sun and good drainage. Don't let them sit in water—they like a quick drink and that's about it. Start with good soil. Add to these some other, more esoteric herbs like marjoram, chives, and savory, and you're well stocked.

Seasonal herbs like cilantro, parsley, dill, mint, and tarragon are typically planted in the spring or fall, depending on the climate, and will grow until it becomes too hot, though, in some locales, they'll grow year-round. It gets really hot where I live and these herbs are usually done for by June, but this is when basil comes in. Buy basil varieties with small leaves. These tend to be more fragrant, sweeter, and less bitter.

CRAB : SIMPLICITY DEFINED

We get a bit of sleep and head out the next day in search of blue crabs. I want pasta with butter and crabs, so we'll need about six big ones to make that work. We wait for low tide, which coincides with our schedule, and head out with the crab gear.

"Crab gear" being a bit of an overstatement: you need string, weights, a net, and a bucket for the crabs. A one-time investment gets you a lifetime of crabbing. It is simplicity defined and possibly one of the best ways to pass an afternoon at the coast, particularly if you have kids. Bait is the universal chicken thigh or neck, and the local grocery store actually has a section in the meat department just for "crab bait."

We head back toward the mainland and choose a likely spot under a bridge where a meager channel cuts from one bay to another. I scarcely have the first chicken thigh flung twenty feet in front of me when it begins walking off at a crab pace. Slowly, I twist the string in my left hand and bend down, burying the long-handled net in the mud between myself and the crab, hoping to pull it and the bait over the hidden net. I inch the greedy crab toward me and scoop it up in the net, where it angrily flails its fat, meaty claws at me. It goes in the bucket.

In less than thirty minutes, our first catch is joined by five of its brethren and we have the makings of the pasta. Jody congratulates me on my efficiency in gathering food and we head back to quickly boil the crabs and laboriously extract their sweet meat from their shells. We will boil the pasta in the water used to boil the crabs to give it more flavor and stretch our precious protein.

Picking Crabs

Tools needed: a nutcracker, a small hammer, or pliers; and a small butter knife

1 Turn the crab upside down and pull its "tail" away from the body. Remove the tail.

2 Pull the top shell down and away. Remove any of the spongy lung left on the body.

3 Remove the two large claws and all the smaller claws and set aside.

4 Break the crab's body in two.

5 Break each half in half again. Carefully remove all the meat from the quartered body and place it in a bowl.

6 Crack the large claws with a nutcracker, or lightly hit them with a hammer. Avoid breaking the shell in a lot of places. Using your hands, break the claws open and remove the claw meat.

7 Break the next segment of the claw and remove the meat, using a small knife if needed. Crack and remove the meat from the other small claws, if desired.

8 Picked crabmeat ready for your recipe.

Crab Posole

This soup stretches precious crabmeat with hominy, dried herbs, chili, and spices. The addition of raw shredded cabbage, radishes, cilantro, and limes at the end covers the entire flavor spectrum and makes this soup well worth the effort. Try this for brunch.

6 to 8 live blue crabs

1 head garlic, halved

2 tablespoons kosher salt, plus additional
  for seasoning

2 tablespoons olive oil

3 onions, chopped

6 garlic cloves, thinly sliced

1 bunch cilantro, stems and leaves
  separated and chopped

4 poblano peppers, seeded and chopped

1 tablespoon Mexican oregano

2 bay leaves

1 teaspoon dried thyme

1 pound tomatillos, chopped

Four 6-inch corn tortillas

One 29-ounce can white hominy, drained

½ small head green cabbage, very thinly sliced

6 radishes, thinly sliced

3 serrano peppers, finely chopped

4 Key limes, quartered

Serves 4

1. Rinse the crabs well under cold running water.

2. In a large pot, bring 2 gallons of water, the halved garlic, and the 2 tablespoons salt to a boil over high heat. Add the crabs and lower to a simmer. Cook for 5 minutes, then turn off the heat and allow the crabs to sit in the water for another 5 minutes.

3. Remove the crabs and let cool, strain and reserve the cooking liquid. Pick the meat from the crabs (page 94). Set aside the meat in the refrigerator.

4. In another large pot, heat the olive oil over medium heat and add the onions, sliced garlic, cilantro stems, poblanos, oregano, bay leaves, and thyme. Cook, stirring occasionally, until softened, about 15 minutes.

5. Add the tomatillos and tortillas and cook for 10 minutes longer.

6. Add the hominy and 8 cups of the reserved crab cooking liquid. Bring to a simmer and cook for 5 minutes, or until hot and slightly thickened.

7. Add the picked crabmeat to the soup and season with salt. Serve in large bowls with the cabbage, radishes, serranos, cilantro leaves, and lime wedges on the side.

Pasta with Crab, Basil, and Garlic

This is a great way to stretch a few crabs; you get some of the rich meat, toss it with pasta that's been boiled in the crab cooking liquid, and add simple, flattering ingredients for a filling dish. Substitute picked blue crabmeat if you don't have fresh crabs, and feel free to use as much crab as you desire.

6 to 8 live blue crabs

2 tablespoons kosher salt, plus more for seasoning

1 pound high-quality dried or fresh linguini, spaghetti, or other pasta

4 tablespoons unsalted butter, softened

6 garlic cloves, minced

¼ cup fresh basil leaves, torn

Crushed red pepper flakes

Zest of 1 lemon

Serves 2

1. Rinse the crabs well under cold running water.

2. In a large pot, bring 2 gallons of water and the 2 tablespoons salt to a boil over high heat. Add the crabs and lower to a simmer. Cook for 5 minutes, then turn off the heat and allow the crabs to sit in the water for another 5 minutes.

3. Remove the crabs and let cool, reserving the cooking liquid. Pick the meat from the crabs (page 94). Set aside the meat in the refrigerator.

4. Strain the cooking liquid and bring to a boil. Add the pasta and cook just until tender.

5. While the pasta is cooking, warm a large bowl over it and add the picked crab, butter, garlic, basil, a bit of red pepper flakes, and the lemon zest.

6. Drain the cooked pasta well and add it to the warmed bowl. Toss, season with salt, and serve immediately.

Feral Hog

THE HOG HIGHWAY

We made the decision late last night to ascend Creepy Canyon before first light this morning, and morning has come too quickly at Madroño Ranch. Morgan, our camp chef, is determined to get a hog, and this may be the last opportunity before we leave the ranch. In the predawn, pre-coffee blur, I show some bemusement at the nice sweater, white shirt, and magenta pants she has chosen for something that could—hopefully—get messy, but she always makes good decisions and I don't push it beyond a couple of sideways glances. Anyway, it doesn't matter—everyone is tired from a long weekend of guiding others on hog hunts, and butchering and cooking pigs, plus the night before had been the typical, cathartic guests-are-gone staff party, complete with wine, and we are both feeling it.

We park the truck at the base of the canyon, next to a very popular feeder, and immediately see a couple of pigs that are, unfortunately, moving too fast for us to get a shot. There is an energy in the just-cool April air, and there are hogs everywhere.

Creepy Canyon is a one-way road winding up through impossibly steep limestone hillsides scattered with juniper, oak, and the odd madrone. A sycamore-lined dry creek bed below parallels the rocky road. So steep are its sides that the creek only sees sunlight for a few hours a day. Along this streambed is a path that looks like it was built by Boy Scouts, but was actually forged by feral hogs, en masse. It is obviously well traveled and three to four feet wide in parts—the Hog Highway.

The Hog Highway leads to the terminus of the road and the confluence of two wet-weather creek beds, with a small turnaround, just big enough for a truck to pass around the feeder that dominates this only flat spot in the whole area. A dilapidated blind sits a preposterous twenty paces away from the feeder,

with its back door exposed to the Hog Highway. In a blind like this you can tell other hunters things like "Aim for the pupil," "You might have to shoot your way out," or "Bring a sidearm," with some humor but little irony. It is a close-quarters situation, and you never quite get past the feeling that you are in the pigs' home, and that you are indeed surrounded. It's like being in enemy territory.

Having chosen to stalk the road and the scree-covered hillsides to our left and right, we can already hear the hogs rooting in several locations as we approach the flat. Rocks and pebbles, dislodged by traveling pigs, tumble down the cliffs, though not at a pace or frenzy that suggests that the pigs are fleeing. They're just going about their morning routine.

They are oblivious to our approach, so far. We walk very slowly, scanning the road and rocks for black shapes in the emerging light, but see nothing. It is still too dark. I take the .270 from Morgan just to see if there's enough light being gathered by the scope to take a shot.

I opt to wait the last couple of minutes before we round that final corner of the road, where most of the rooting noises are coming from. I know that the hogs' poor eyesight won't alert them, and that the gentle north breeze blowing straight down the canyon into our faces means they can't smell us either, even if one of us is wearing angora and we both smell like red wine. The birds begin to flit about and call to one another and the canyon becomes two shades lighter.

Morgan again has the rifle, and I tell her to walk along the right side of the road, slowly, until we've rounded the bend. We take careful, soft steps, heel to toe, making sure that we don't ruin the long walk in by crushing a twig or stepping into a pile of dry leaves and triggering an alert: hogs have a keen sense of hearing. I am now five paces behind her, creeping along at an extremely slow speed, bringing the flat into view by the inch. We can see the crooked blind and the trees ringing the flat, and the rocks on the road, glowing white like limestone does sometimes in transitional light. Then, there it is: a black shape, and another.

I tap her shoulder and whisper in the lowest of voices to take good aim, but shoot and shoot now. "The one on the right," I say. "The big one." She is standing and takes the freehand shot before I am ready, because you are never quite ready for someone else to take a shot. I am watching through my binoculars as the bigger pig on the right squeals mournfully, turns, and runs to the left, straight up a steep slope through a tangle of juniper. I am certain it is a hit. We wait a few minutes, then slowly proceed to the flat and search for blood. Nothing, not a drop. Plenty of pig dung and uneaten corn and peas, but no blood. Then, we hear it.

It's a wheezing coming from up the slope, up the thin paths that crisscross and switch back through the juniper thickets and piles of leaves that line the cliffs. This sound carries on for a minute, then stops. Now I know it was a hit. We start up the hillside, scrambling and climbing while carrying rifles, without any blood trail to follow, looking for a lifeless black heap. After a few minutes, we reach the top of the hill, dejected at our prospects of finding the animal. We're about to turn back when I spot the pig, lying innocuously about fifteen feet from where I stand at the base of a gnarled juniper, stone dead.

For a few seconds, I can't even believe it is her pig, and not some other dead pig, but it is still warm and obviously recently shot. We are elated, and drag the carcass down the steep slope, over boulders and sharp limbs to the flat. Winded, Morgan thanks the pig, field dresses it in the now sunny morning, and hardly gets any blood on her white shirt at all.

This pig, a midsize "Madroño special," will be used for braising, roasting, and grilling. Dressing out to about thirty pounds or so, it is a very typical, average-size pig that lacks exterior fat, but will be flavorful and tender if cooked correctly. The tiny chops can be brined and smothered (page 112) or grilled (page 116); the belly can be prepared in the same way as the stuffed venison flank (page 166); the shoulders braised with tomatoes (page 194); and the hams brined and smoked, or boned out for some sausage with a bit of added pork fat. The larger, fattier pigs are the ones we use for curing. If we find one, Morgan will use it to make her prosciutto, pancetta, and dry-cured sausages. Maybe next time.

Field Dressing Large Game

Field dressing—or cleaning the animal in the field—is the first step taken after the shot, typically. If you do not have fast access to gambrels (The Gambrel Method, page 156), or the animal is gut shot, then it is a necessity. Intestinal damage increases the chance of spoilage, and any damaged viscera should be removed as soon as possible to prevent contamination. Field dressing also cools animals faster by removing the internal organs, makes them lighter for transport, and leaves unwanted innards disposed of in the field.

Tools needed: a small, sharp knife, such as a pocketknife or boning knife; a small handheld bone saw for cutting through the pelvis of a larger animal; another person to hold the carcass (helpful but not imperative)

1 Find an area to work in, preferably with a slight slope, and position the animal with its head higher than its hindquarters.

2 If it's a male, remove the penis by lifting and cutting just under the skin all the way back to the anus, using the tip of the knife to cut under the urinary tract, but not into the stomach cavity.

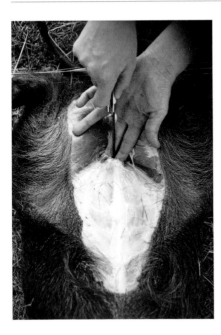

3 Between the two back legs and just forward of the pelvic bone, make a small and shallow incision with the tip of the knife. Insert the index and middle fingers of your other hand into the cut and place the knife blade, blade side up, between your two fingers.

4 Using the fingers as a guide, cut the animal's underside open, lifting the skin up to prevent any viscera from being cut.

5 Forcefully cut along either side of the sternum in the center of the chest cavity, through the softer cartilage. Make the cut all the way to the animal's chin.

6 The animal is ready to be gutted.

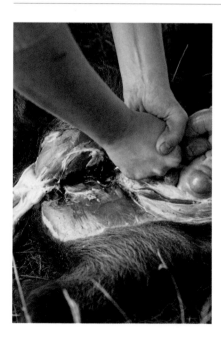

7 On a smaller animal, a knife can be used to break and cut through the pelvic bone between the legs. Place the knife, blade facing upward, under the pelvic bone and pop it upward forcefully. If using a small bone saw, simply cut through the pelvic bone in the center.

8 Force both legs downward, splitting the pelvis open.

9 Use the tip of the knife to free the intestines around the anus; when the guts are removed, the intestinal tract will come out with them.

10 Sever the trachea at the animal's throat. Now, all of the viscera from the neck to the anus have been freed and are ready to be pulled out.

11 Grip the trachea and pull back toward the hind legs, removing the lungs and heart.

12 Use the knife to free any connective tissue holding the guts in while pulling everything out in one mass.

13 The gutted animal, ready for skinning.

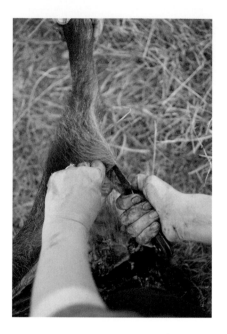

14 With the knife blade facing upward, cut through the skin of a back leg to the hoof.

15 Running the blade of the knife between the flesh and the skin, begin pulling and cutting the skin away from the body on one side of the animal.

16 Continue along the side of the animal, removing the skin all the way to the backbone.

17 Repeat on the other side.

18 Lift the animal and cut all the way around the head behind the ears, all the way to the bone.

19 Twist the head off, pulling downward. If working alone, cut the head off with a bone saw.

20 The finished carcass, ready. Cool this down quickly and dispose of the viscera and skin responsibly.

Butchering a Feral Hog

Hogs have a very generous amount of meat and are easy to butcher. For the smaller pigs, I use a simple cleaver-and-mallet technique that works well. I place the cleaver where I want it and then hit it with a rubber mallet to get it where I want it to go. Add a sharp boning knife and you have all the tools you need to convert a skinned pig into myriad cuts. For bigger sows and boars, a bone saw is necessary for making some major cuts, but always use a knife to cut through flesh and then use the saw or cleaver to cut through bone.

Deer can be butchered the same way; use this method on a deer for obtaining the racks and chops. Conversely, use the method of removing the loins from a deer (page 164) to take off the loins from a hog. These loins can be cleaned of all silverskin and cooked over a hot grill, or thinly sliced and pounded for cutlets (page 189).

Tools needed: a cleaver and mallet, a sharp boning knife, and a bone saw (for larger hogs)

A. Hams
Brine and smoke, braise, or bone out for sausage.

B. Belly
On larger hogs, use for Pancetta (page 126), Salted Wild Boar Belly (page 134) or substitute for Stuffed Venison Flank (page 166).

C. Trim
Use for sausage or stew.

D. Saddle
Brine and roast or smoke whole.

E. Chops and Rack
Left side: chops. Brine and grill over a hot fire. Right side: rack. Brine and grill or smoke. Don't overcook.

F. Ribs
See Cheater Ribs (page 116).

G. Shoulder
Braise or bone out for sausage.

H. Spare Ribs
On smaller hogs use for stock. On larger hogs see Cheater Ribs (page 116).

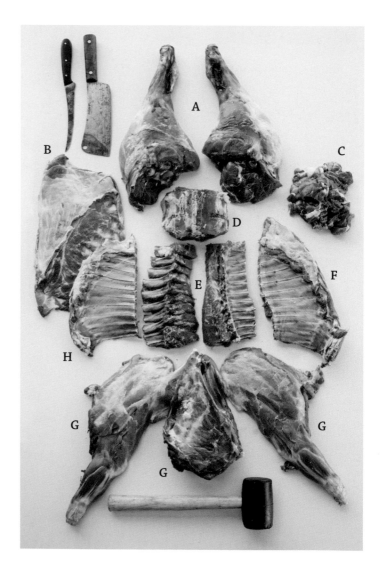

1 Where the back legs meet the body, make a cut all the way around the hog with the boning knife. On larger pigs, remove the tenderloins, found on the inside of the body cavity, as with deer (page 164).

2 Place the cleaver at this cut and, using the mallet, cut through the bone, separating the back legs from the body.

3 Remove the hams by cutting down to the ball-and-socket joint at the hip. Use the tip of the knife to cut around the ball, then cut against the pelvic bone to remove the entire ham. Trim the meat from the triangular piece left from cutting off the hams.

4 Remove the shoulders: holding a front leg in one hand, follow the natural contour of the joint, cutting along the wide, round shoulder blade where it meets the body. Completely separate the shoulder from the carcass, and repeat with the other shoulder.

5 Looking into the cavity, locate the third and fourth ribs down from the top of the rib cage and cut between them with the knife, then use the cleaver to cut through the bones.

6 Make a cut through the meat just under the loin—an oval-shaped muscle running along either side of the spine, forming the top third of this middle section, and containing the chops.

7 With the tip of a sharp knife, trim the belly meat away from the ribs. Take care to cut around the white cartilage at the bottom of the ribs.

8 Alternatively, for a rack of ribs, leave this belly piece on, trimming the flap at the end of the ribs.

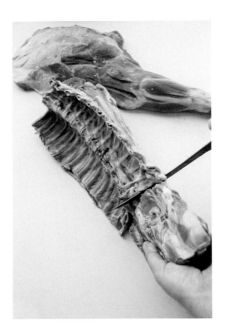

9 Remove the rib bones: following the cut under the loin, use either the cleaver and mallet or bone saw to cut through the ribs.

10 With the knife, then the cleaver, cut all the way around the loin just behind the last rib, forming the saddle. The loin on either side of this cut can be removed and trimmed of all sinew.

11 Using the two removed shoulders to hold the rack in place, use the tip of the cleaver and the mallet to cut through the rib bones right where they meet the spine. Work carefully and just cut through the bone. Repeat on the other side.

12 Following the spine, cut the loins away, resulting in two racks of pork. Cut into chops if desired.

Smothered Boar Chops

Browning fatty chops, then slow-cooking them with lots and lots of sweet onion, results in tender, flavorful pork and an incredibly savory gravy—scented by the anise brine—that should be served over plain rice or mashed potatoes. I wouldn't serve smothered chops without Braised Greens (page 27), either. This recipe works well with chops of all sizes, including tiny ones from 30-pound pigs to the big boar chops from a giant feral hog. Some chops may need a bit more cooking, so plan accordingly.

8 bone-in boar chops from a medium-size hog (more or less if using smaller or larger chops)

1 recipe Anise Brine (below)

4 tablespoons lard or oil

1 cup all-purpose flour

8 onions, thinly sliced

1 bay leaf

Kosher salt and freshly ground black pepper

1 gallon Feral Hog Stock (page 173), **chicken stock, or water**

Serves 4

1. Brine the chops for 12 hours in a nonreactive container in the refrigerator, then remove and pat dry with paper towels.

2. Preheat the oven to 325°F.

3. In a large ovenproof pot or Dutch oven, heat the lard or oil over medium heat. Dredge the chops in the flour, shaking off the excess. Reserve the left-over flour.

4. Brown the chops very well in the fat, about 4 minutes per side, and transfer to a plate. Reduce the heat to medium-low. Add the onions and bay leaf and cook, stirring often, until the onions are softened, about 15 minutes. Season with salt and pepper.

5. Add 6 tablespoons of the flour to the onions and stir well. Slowly add the stock, stirring and scraping the pan well, until all of the stock is incorporated and the mixture is slightly thickened.

6. Return the chops to the pan, bring to a simmer, cover tightly, and bake in the oven until tender, 2 or more hours. Serve the chops with plenty of gravy over rice or mashed potatoes.

Anise Brine

The sweetness of brown sugar and the subtle flavor of star anise meld beautifully with feral hogs. We brine everything from little chops to whole pigs in this.

6 ounces kosher salt

1 cup packed brown sugar

2 star anise

4 bay leaves

Makes 1 gallon

In a large pot, heat 1 gallon of water and all of the ingredients over high heat until the sugar and salt are dissolved. Let cool completely and refrigerate until needed.

Wild Boar Carnitas

Fatty, crisp, and chewy, "little meats" make a perfect taco with raw onion and fresh cilantro. The meat is browned slowly and cooked until tender in the oven. Use lard if the pig is a bit lean, or try to make this with fatty cuts—i.e., belly—from fatty hogs. The long cooking time of this recipe lends itself well to an overnighter in the oven. Serve carnitas with beer and stacks of good tortillas, and Jalapeño Salsa (recipe below).

2 pounds fatty hog belly or shoulder, diced

Kosher salt

1 teaspoon ground cumin

1 teaspoon Mexican oregano

¼ teaspoon ground coriander

2 teaspoons guajillo or chipotle chile powder

1 teaspoon freshly ground black pepper

Juice and zest of 1 orange

Serves 4

1. Preheat the oven to 225°F.

2. In an ovenproof pot or Dutch oven, combine all of the ingredients and stir to combine. Cover the pot tightly, place in the oven, and cook until very tender and crisp, about 6 to 7 hours. If the carnitas are still not deeply browned, place the pot over high heat and cook, stirring often, for a few minutes until the pieces caramelize nicely.

Jalapeño Salsa

Modeled after the house salsa at the Meson Principal in Saltillo, Mexico, this salsa is super-simple, but perfect. I was shocked to taste such a good sauce made from only three ingredients.

8 large ripe tomatoes

2 to 4 jalapeño peppers

Kosher salt

Makes about 1 pint

1. Build a hot fire or preheat a grill or broiler.

2. Char the tomatoes and peppers very well—there should be plenty of black on the tomatoes and pepper skins. Remove the tomatoes and peppers from the heat and let cool.

3. Remove the stems from the peppers and the cores from the tomatoes and discard. Place the peppers and tomatoes in the bowl of a food processor and pulse until still coarse (or smooth if you prefer). Season with salt.

Cheater Ribs

"Cheater" because the ribs are first cooked in simmering water, then simply crisped over a hot grill with a sweet glaze instead of laboriously smoking or grilling. This method also yields a nice spiced broth that can be frozen for later use in a soup or for cooking beans. We recommend using ribs from larger hogs for this—they have more fat and more substance in general, though we've had ribs from 30-pound hogs that were pretty good, although small.

2 racks of wild boar ribs or venison ribs

Kosher salt and freshly ground black pepper

2 bay leaves

1 hot pepper, such as a serrano or jalapeño

1 star anise

2 whole juniper berries

1 teaspoon anise seed

1 onion, peeled

1 head garlic, halved

½ cup honey

½ cup vinegar

Olive oil, for brushing

Serves 4 to 8, depending on size of ribs

1. Season the ribs with salt and pepper and refrigerate for 24 hours.

2. To a large pot, add the ribs, bay leaves, hot pepper, spices, onion, and garlic and cover with cold water by about 6 inches. Bring to a boil over high heat, lower to a simmer, and cook until tender, 2 to 4 hours, depending on the age of the animal. Add water, as needed, to keep the ribs submerged.

3. Remove the ribs, let cool, and refrigerate. Strain the broth, let cool, and refrigerate for another use, in soups or for cooking beans, rice, or lentils.

4. Make a hot fire in a charcoal grill, or set a gas grill on high heat.

5. Mix together the honey and vinegar. Brush the ribs with olive oil and season again with a little salt and pepper.

6. Grill the ribs until browned on one side, about 4 minutes. Brush with the honey and vinegar mixture and grill for about 1 minute, being careful not to burn the glaze. Repeat for the opposite side. Repeat this process several times more, until the ribs are nicely glazed and falling apart, about 10 minutes.

7. Transfer the ribs to a cutting board and cut them apart. Serve immediately.

Wild Boar Petit Salé

This is a good way to make both salted wild boar belly and lentils shine. The salty pork is poached until tender, making a rich broth, and then the lentils are cooked in the poaching liquid with spices and sweet carrots. Served with pickled onions to cut the richness, this is a classic, hearty pork-legume pairing. Classically, this country French dish would be made with fat, domesticated pork belly, or maybe a salted (salé) bit of shoulder, but a fat belly from a large feral boar or sow stands in nicely.

Pickled Onions (below)

2 pounds Salted Wild Boar Belly in one piece (page 134)

2 onions, 1 halved and 1 finely diced

2 carrots, finely diced

5 whole allspice berries

¼ teaspoon cumin seed

2 cups dried French green lentils

Kosher salt and freshly ground black pepper

Serves 4

1. Prepare the Pickled Onions the day before.

2. In a large pot, combine 3 gallons of water, the belly, and halved onion and bring to a simmer over high heat. Lower the heat and simmer until tender, about 5 hours, adding water, as needed, to keep the belly submerged.

3. Remove the belly and set aside. Strain the stock and discard the onion.

4. In another pot, combine the diced onion, carrots, allspice, cumin, lentils, and 6 cups of the reserved stock. Bring to a simmer over high heat, lower the flame, and simmer the lentils until tender, about 30 minutes, adding more broth, if necessary. Season with salt and pepper.

5. Preheat the broiler. Place the belly in a pan, fatty side up, and broil until slightly crisp, about 2 minutes. Slice the belly against the grain and serve over the lentils with some pickled onions on top.

Pickled Onions

These crunchy and sour pickles will last for a month or more in the refrigerator, and go well with grilled meats or fatty cuts.

1 large onion, very thinly sliced

1 cup apple cider vinegar

1 teaspoon kosher salt

2 tablespoons sugar

2 whole cloves

1 teaspoon dried thyme

Makes 2 pints

1. Place the onion in a glass, plastic, or ceramic container.

2. In a pot, combine 1 cup of water and the rest of the ingredients. Bring to a boil over high heat. Remove from heat and pour the hot liquid over the onions.

3. Cover the container tightly, let cool, and refrigerate for at least a day before using.

Roasted Whole Baby Hog

Tender, lean piglets roast beautifully whole and are what we really want to see when we come to check the traps. If you have access to a processor that can "scrape" hogs, or remove the hair and keep the skin on, do this by all means—the crisp skin will almost shatter when slowly cooked over fire. Otherwise, just roast the skinned pig as is and baste often. Use a rotisserie for this, or simply smoke the pig in a smoker, running at 225°F to 250°F. A low oven at 225°F for 6 to 8 hours will also work if you turn the piglet periodically, and baste with olive oil.

2 to 4 gallons Anise Brine, extra strong: see step 1

A whole baby pig, 8 to 15 pounds, dressed

10 sprigs rosemary

1 to 2 cups olive oil, for brushing

Freshly ground black pepper

Serves about 1 person per pound of pig

1. Make the Anise Brine (page 112) extra strong: use 3 cups of salt to 2 gallons of water. Let cool completely.

2. Put the pig in a small cooler and cover with the brine. Brine the pig for 24 hours—adding a couple of bags of ice (about 20 pounds) over the duration. This will keep the brine sufficiently cold without diluting it. Remove the pig and dry well with towels.

3. Start a fire under the rotisserie. I like to use charcoal—pure lump oak charcoal or mesquite—for heat and wood for smoke and flavor. Build two small fires parallel to the rotisserie rod and let the charcoal burn down to white coals. Add a handful of small branches or soaked wood chips.

4. Place the pig on the rotisserie rod. Tie the rosemary sprigs to the handle end of a wooden spoon and use to baste the pig with olive oil. Begin turning the pig on the rotisserie. Put the lid on (if available) and open the air vents all the way. Baste the pig with olive oil, using the rosemary sprigs, and season with black pepper, about every 30 minutes. Add more wood by the handful about every 30 minutes to keep the fire hot and smoky.

5. Spin the pig for about 6 to 8 hours, depending on size, until very tender and a meat thermometer registers 155°F to 160°F when inserted in the thickest part of the leg and the shoulder right behind the head.

6. Once the meat is tender, let the fire die down, and keep the pig turning on the spit—this is a great way to rest the meat, as it stays in motion and bastes itself, keeping the juices in the flesh. Add just enough wood to keep the pig warm.

7. Serve the pig whole on a platter with roasted potatoes and a very simple salad or Braised Greens (page 27), with a great, rough wine and bread. Use tongs to pull the meat from the bone, and a sharp knife to cut the crisp skin and larger pieces like the legs and loin from the pig.

Sausage & Charcuterie

A NICE FAT SOW

"What are them black spots down in that pasture?" asks Tink. Pigs, and lots of them. Tink can spot animals a mile away. Literally: he just did. He can also see them at night, standing in the brush behind him. When you've been guiding for twenty years (or twenty-five, depending on wine consumption), you get the "critter vision."

We had been scouting the ranch for the entire afternoon, more as a reconnoitering trip for our hunt next month than an actual hunt, but still, I needed a pig. A big, fat one for

curing. Morgan had placed the order so she could make pancetta and salted pork belly, and so far we had just shot lots of Madroño specials—perfectly good, smaller wild pigs, but in the thirty- to fifty-pounds range. We already had several of these hanging in the cooler, and were now prepared to pass on anything except a very large one with fatty potential—one that would make a beautiful pancetta, laced with streaks of deep red lean meat and soft white fat.

Through my binoculars, I can only tell that there is a big black animal way down in the pasture on the far northern corner of the property, surrounded by other black animals. We are perched on the steep incline of a rocky road at the top of a hill just to the south, about a ten-minute drive to the paddock below. We lurch forward at a creeping pace down the mountain, silently hoping that the pigs stay put long enough for us to stalk them.

The plan of attack is simple. The large grassy flat where the pigs are feeding lies above a creek flanked with oaks, cottonwood, sycamore, and a couple of towering cypress trees. A narrow road cuts through this tree line at an angle and crosses the pasture, and I only need to move slowly up this road, screened by the trees, to get up on these hogs. The north wind will be in my face, making this even better, because my human scent is the only thing that could spook them now.

Finally, we are at the bottom of the craggy hill and pull up to the gate about five hundred yards from the flat. I undo the chain and it clangs about loudly; I curse under my breath. Josh hops out of the truck and follows behind me with his binoculars while I load three rounds into the .270.

I'm down in the creek bottom now and completely out of view of the pigs, so they could be gone by now, but at least they can't see me. I creep up the right side of the road and, walking heel to toe, inch my way up the road, each step exposing a bit more of the gently sloping pasture. At first, I see nothing. Then I see the heads and white tails of five whitetail does, which I momentarily consider but ignore—I need that fat pig.

I drop to my belly and crawl very slowly up the embankment, aware that I am crawling through a lot of pig sign, which is oddly encouraging and disconcerting at the same time. I can hear them. I hit the apex of the subtle slope and now see black shapes everywhere, feeding excitedly and oblivious to my presence. I start counting, but soon forget my count when I see her.

She is a giant fat sow, and this is working out perfectly. I can't tell exactly how large she is, but she is a hell of a lot bigger than any of the others on the flat, and definitely the black shape we saw from above.

The deer snort, flick their tails, and start to scamper off. They've no doubt seen me, as I'm only fifty feet away at this point and not concealed by so much as a bush. This registers as a message to act quickly, as the pigs may pick up on the deer's nervousness and run. The hillside across from me is very steep but well traveled, and will be their obvious escape route should they get spooked or if I need to make a follow-up shot.

I raise the gun and slowly sit up. The pigs are still completely unaware of me. The closest one is thirty feet away, noisily rooting in the wet ground. The big sow is also feeding actively, moving a lot. I place the crosshairs on her ear—I'm taking no chances and wasting no precious shoulder—and apply pressure to the trigger. A shoulder shot worries me, as a pig this large has extremely tough skin, and my bullet has to pass through two thick shoulder blades. A smaller pig bolts in front of her and I pause.

Sensing I have a few more moments while they feed frantically, I lie prostrate and find her again in my scope. I'm able to steady it more with my elbows on the ground, and I line her up again. She turns toward me and I consider a frontal shot, right between the eyes and a little high, but wait instead for her to expose the side of her head and spine. It looks as if she's looking right at me, and I'm nervous that another pig may run my way at any second.

She turns left and the crosshairs find her ear. I have to dial the reticle of the scope back because she is so close that she takes up the whole scope. I don't even hear the shot when I fire, but know she is down, and down for good. A dozen or two black pigs immediately run, squealing, through the fence and up the trail, but she is lying right where she should, and I know we have our fat pig.

Tink backs the truck all the way up—there's no way we can carry this pig—and we one, two, three swing her up, feeling her weight. Tink is grinning from ear to ear and estimates her weight at just under 200 pounds. As he was the guide of a successful stalk, the pig on the ground is just as much his doing as mine.

Hanging her up at the gambrels, I feel almost blessed by this pig. She is exactly what we wanted. She is also kind of pretty in a piggish way, dark gray brown instead of black, and dignified-looking. With as much

hatred as there is out there for pigs, I always have great respect for their ability to survive, and even thrive, anywhere. Tough, intelligent, and quick to learn, they can be damn hard to hunt. And the benefits: these wild pigs are delicious, coming in different sizes and varying in fat content. The tiny piglets caught in the traps can be brined and spun on a rotisserie, while the medium-size ones contribute beautiful roasts and smaller hams for quicker, impatient curing.

This one, however, looks like it could have been a domestic pig, and I painstakingly skin her to keep as much fat attached as possible. We will need to add no extra pork fat to the dry-cured sausages, and the belly is streaked with a two-inch-thick cap of pure fat.

Transforming wild meat into beautiful bacons, sausages, and terrines is a practice built from necessity. It was once a way to preserve the food, and now is more of a way to make it shine. Morgan makes several prosciutti every year from hogs we shoot, and she heads up the curing of the spicy dried sausages, the bresaola, and the pancetta.

She has converted an old restaurant refrigerator into her curing cellar, which works surprisingly well. Even a small dorm fridge or wine cooler can be used, as long as it can hold a high temperature of about 60°F consistently. Humidity is also important in drying. A relative humidity of around 60 percent is optimal, so that the outside of the cured meat doesn't dry out and instead forms an impenetrable barrier to the inside, which slows the drying. A slow, monitored drying is the goal. Besides this, keeping everything spotlessly sanitized is key. These are meats that are not cooked, but salted and dried.

Other recipes in this section require no more specialized equipment than a meat grinder and a sausage stuffer, and maybe add a smoker. Refer to Making Sausage (page 136) for more tips and instruction. Then get your wild game, make big batches of goods, and invite some friends over to share in the bounty.

Morgan's Wild Boar Pancetta

The cured, musty, salty flavor of pancetta can elevate a dish, like a bowl of carbonara, Braised Greens (page 27), or a pot of beans. Slice it thinly and crisp it in the oven for salads, or add it to sandwiches or burgers. Use the bellies from larger feral hogs with a good amount of fat—I would say that they need to be at least 150 pounds live weight to even be considered for this or Salted Wild Boar Belly (page 134), otherwise they will be too thin and lean. Hogs taken at the end of winter, or from areas with a bountiful food source like acorns, have often put on more fat and make better pancetta.

---

2 teaspoons Insta Cure No. 2*

2 tablespoons dark brown sugar

2 ounces kosher salt

4 cinnamon sticks

2 tablespoons crushed juniper berries

4 bay leaves

4 teaspoons fennel seed

4 tablespoons whole black peppercorns

1 large feral hog belly, about 5 pounds, squared off and trimmed

2 tablespoons pâté spice (page 131)

4 garlic cloves, minced

6 sprigs thyme

Makes about 3½ pounds

1. Combine the Insta Cure, brown sugar, and kosher salt in a small bowl and set aside. Toast the cinnamon sticks, juniper, bay leaves, and fennel seed in a dry pan over medium heat for one minute, then remove to a small bowl. Once they are cool, crush the bay leaves and juniper berries. Meanwhile, in the same pan, toast the peppercorns. When cool, place them in a plastic bag and crush with a meat mallet or the bottom of a heavy pan; divide in half and set aside. Rub the whole belly on both sides with the Insta Cure mixture first, then just the rib side with the pâté spice. Add the garlic and half of the black pepper to the rib side. Place the belly in a large, sealable freezer bag, and add the toasted spices and fresh thyme. Make sure to leave some air in the bag when you seal it, to allow the resulting brine to move around. Refrigerate for 6 to 7 days, turning every other day. Check for firmness. If it still feels soft, allow to cure for 1 to 2 more days.

2. Remove the belly from the bag, rinse under cold water, pat very dry and sprinkle the rib-side with the remaining cracked pepper.

3. Lay out a length of cheesecloth that will cover the whole belly with at least a 2-inch overhang at the top and bottom. Lay the belly on top of the cloth and roll it into itself with the skin/fat side out. Tightly tie each end, then tie tightly at 4-inch increments. Leave one long tag end for hanging. Hang the pancetta for 2 to 3 weeks in a refrigerator or wine cooler to dry, ideally at 50° to 60°F, with a relative humidity of 60%.**

4. Testing for readiness: after the second week it should start to firm up, but will probably be a little soft yet—you'll know it's ready when it is quite firm to the touch but not hard as a rock. When ready, wrap it in plastic wrap and refrigerate. The pancetta will keep in the refrigerator for up to 3 months.

*Curing salt necessary to inhibit growth of bacteria. Use and store with caution.

**Dry-curing is a temperamental process, dependent on air and humidity, and involves safety and sanitation issues that may deter novices. Safety is important: you can make yourself or someone else very sick with improperly cured meats. Fuzzy or greenish mold is bad. Throw out your cured meat if this develops. If it smells off, or if it is mushy or not dried through, do not eat it.

Venison Bresaola

Bresaola is air-dried beef, but translates to venison extremely well. Use the loin if you're flush with them, or carefully trim out leg muscles and cure these. The juniper berries, coriander, and brown sugar are all complementary to the musty iron flavor of good bresaola, and the black pepper both preserves the venison and contributes heat. We use curing salt in this recipe—Insta Cure No. 2—to retain the rosy color, add flavor, and safely cure this item. Serve the bresaola sliced paper thin, with arugula, and a little lemon or orange zest as a starter, followed by more venison.

**3 pounds venison loin or leg fillets,
   well trimmed**

6 tablespoons whole black peppercorns

3 tablespoons salt

3 tablespoons brown sugar

¾ teaspoon coriander seed

6 whole juniper berries

½ teaspoon Insta Cure No. 2*

Makes 2 pounds

1. In a spice or coffee grinder, coarsely grind the peppercorns, salt, brown sugar, coriander, juniper, and Insta Cure.

2. Rub and coat the venison evenly with this mixture and let cure in the refrigerator for 7 days in an airtight container or bag, turning once a day.

3. Brush the cure off of the venison and wrap each piece in cheesecloth.

4. Tie each piece at 2-inch intervals, leaving a tag end for hanging. Weigh each piece and label with the weight.

5. Hang the venison for 5 to 7 weeks in a refrigerator to dry, ideally at 50° to 60°F, with a relative humidity of 60%. The bresaola is ready when the loin cuts have lost 30 percent of their weight, down to about 2 pounds.**

6. When ready, wrap the bresaola in plastic wrap and refrigerate. To serve, slice very thinly against the grain. The bresaola will keep, refrigerated, for up to 2 months.

*Curing salt necessary to inhibit growth of bacteria. Use and store with caution.

**Dry-curing is a temperamental process, dependent on air and humidity, and involves safety and sanitation issues that may deter novices. Safety is important: you can make yourself or someone else very sick with improperly cured meats. Fuzzy or greenish mold is bad. Throw out your cured meat if this develops. If it smells off, or if it is mushy or not dried through, do not eat it.

Dove Terrine

A terrine, or pâté, is a perfect way to use livers, hearts, and gizzards. Substitute goose, duck, quail, pheasant, or even feral hog or venison liver for the dove livers, and experiment with different liqueurs, too. A couple of handfuls of diced apple, cooked quickly in hot butter, add another dimension to this terrine. Serve the terrine with mustard, grilled bread, and pickles, or even a sweet-and-sour chutney.

4 ounces dove livers, hearts, and cleaned gizzards, cut into 1-inch pieces

8 ounces dove breasts, left whole

4 tablespoons brandy

1 teaspoon olive oil

1 tablespoon unsalted butter

1 onion, sliced

1 teaspoon chopped fresh thyme

1¼ pounds domestic pork or fatty feral hog shoulder, diced

¼ cup bread crumbs

¾ cup heavy cream

2 eggs, beaten

5 teaspoons kosher salt

¼ teaspoon pâté spice*

Serves 6 to 8 as a first course

1. In a large bowl, toss the dove livers, hearts, gizzards, and breasts with the brandy and marinate overnight in the refrigerator.

2. Preheat the oven to 300°F. Brush the inside of a terrine mold or loaf pan with the olive oil.

3. Heat the butter in a small sauté pan over medium heat and cook the onion and thyme until softened, about 10 minutes. Refrigerate the onion mixture.

4. Grind the pork shoulder through the medium plate of a meat grinder into a chilled bowl, then refrigerate.

5. In a large bowl, mix the bread crumbs, cream, and eggs well and let soak for a few minutes, refrigerated. Add the marinated dove pieces, ground pork, onion mixture, salt, and pâté spice, and mix well.

6. Pack the mixture into the terrine mold and cover tightly with aluminum foil. Place terrine in a larger baking pan and add hot water to the larger pan to come halfway up the sides of the terrine. Bake 1½ to 2 hours, or until the internal temperature registers 160°F.

7. Remove the terrine from the oven, take it out of the water bath, and let it cool to room temperature. Cut a piece of cardboard to fit over the top of the terrine mixture and wrap the cardboard in plastic wrap. Place the wrapped cardboard on top, then weigh the mixture down with another mold filled with heavy jars or cans. Refrigerate at least 1 day, preferably 2, and up to 7 days.

8. Remove the weights and run a knife around the sides of the terrine to loosen it. Turn the terrine over onto a cutting board and scrape off any excess fat or gelatin. Cut the terrine into ¼-inch slices with a sharp, thin-bladed knife and serve.

*Pâté spice: Combine 2 tablespoons ground ginger, 2 tablespoons ground cinnamon, 1 tablespoon ground nutmeg, 1 tablespoon ground coriander, 1 tablespoon ground cloves, and 1 tablespoon ground white pepper. Store in an airtight container for up to 6 months.

Goose Liver Pâté

Buttery, rich pâté is a wonderful way to enjoy livers, spread on warm toasted baguettes with some tart pickles and wine. Drambuie, a Scottish liqueur, provides a unique boozy quality to this pâté, but you can substitute brandy, cognac, Calvados, or even sweet white wines with great effect. Any bird liver will work in this recipe, though diver ducks may have strong-flavored, almost fishy livers.

8 tablespoons (1 stick) unsalted butter, cut into pieces

1 onion, thinly sliced

1 sprig thyme

8 ounces goose livers, cleaned of any sinew

3 tablespoons Drambuie or brandy

Kosher salt and freshly ground pepper

1 tablespoon orange juice

½ teaspoon pâté spice (page 131)

Serves 4

1. Melt 1 tablespoon of butter in a sauté pan over low heat and cook the onion and thyme until softened, about 8 minutes. Remove the onion mixture and chill in the refrigerator.

2. Add another tablespoon of butter to the pan, increase the heat to medium, and sauté the livers until cooked through but not browned, about 6 minutes. Add the Drambuie and cook until reduced by 1 half, about a minute. Let cool to room temperature.

3. Purée the livers in a food processor or blender, adding salt, pepper, orange juice, and pâté spice, and process until smooth. Add the remaining butter, piece by piece, and process until smooth. With a firm spatula, push the mousse through a fine-mesh strainer set over a bowl and chill. Serve the pâté within 3 days.

Salted Wild Boar Belly

Choose a fatty belly from a larger hog for this salt pork recipe. Once cured, the belly will keep refrigerated for a week or can be frozen. I like to cut the cured belly into half-pound pieces and freeze them for quick thawing. Use cubes of cured belly to season rice, beans, vinaigrettes, soups, and stews.

1 large feral hog belly, about 5 pounds, trimmed to an even thickness

4 ounces kosher salt

2 teaspoons whole pink peppercorns, crushed

2 teaspoons whole white peppercorns, crushed

2 teaspoons black peppercorns, crushed

1 teaspoon dried marjoram

1 teaspoon dried thyme

4 bay leaves

Makes about 5 pounds

1. In a small bowl, mix together all of the ingredients except the belly. Coat the belly evenly with the cure, place in a ceramic or glass dish, and wrap tightly with plastic wrap. Cure in the refrigerator for 7 days, turning the belly every 2 days.

2. Cut the belly into portions; wrap and refrigerate for up to 7 days or freeze for up to 6 months. To cook, panfry the belly in a little oil over medium-low heat, or use in Fish and Oyster Stew (page 72), Wild Boar Petit Salé (page 119), or Braised Greens (page 27).

Wild Boar Rillettes

Rillettes are a spreadable, rich, and fatty preparation, usually made from pork or waterfowl. If you get a nice, fat feral hog, this easy and delicious recipe is perfect. Cook in a low oven overnight and wake up to the smell of roasting pork. Serve rillettes cold or at room temperature, with mustard and pickles to cut the fat, and with great bread, toasted.

2 pounds fatty pork shoulder or trim

½ ounce kosher salt

1 teaspoon pâté spice (page 131)

¼ cup lard (optional)

Serves 8

1. Preheat the oven to 225°F.

2. In a Dutch oven or ovenproof pot, combine the pork, salt, pâté spice, and enough water to cover three-quarters of the meat. Cook, covered, in the oven, for 8 hours or overnight.

3. Remove from the oven and allow to cool slightly. Shred the meat with a wooden spoon, mashing it up well and stirring it to combine with any liquid in the pot.

4. Pack the mixture into a glass or ceramic jar and refrigerate for up to 7 days. If you want to store the rillettes for a couple of weeks, melt the lard and pour it over the cooled rillettes, making sure to cover them completely. Store in the refrigerator for up to 2 weeks. To serve, scrape away the fat and spread the rillettes on toast.

Making Sausage

Making sausage is a classic way to use game meats, and rightly so. Sausages stretch the available proteins, add savor, and are easy to store and cook. A simple game sausage can utilize scrap meats yet still convey the great flavors of game animals. The process, though uncomplicated, takes some time and attention, but since sausages can be made in large batches, it is well worth the effort.

Keep everything as cold as possible. Put the grinder in the freezer, chill the mixing bowls, and partially freeze the meats. This ensures a better texture and is a safer, more sanitary environment for making sausage. Optimally, the meats for grinding are partially frozen while being ground, and are returned to the freezer if they're to be ground again.

BASIC EQUIPMENT

Grinder

A good, powerful grinder will make life easier if you are making a couple of large batches a year. Spend the money on a quality grinder with stainless parts and a strong motor. You will need at least two dies, medium and small, to start. These regulate the size of the grind and impart different textures to the sausage.

Mixer

A small KitchenAid mixer with a paddle attachment is great for mixing sausages, but this can also be accomplished by hand.

Stuffer

I highly recommend a hand-cranked stuffer, which makes filling the casings go very quickly and does not overwork the meat once it is ground. This is not an absolute necessity, but again, will be a good investment over many seasons. A 5- to 15-pound canister is more than adequate.

Tools

A sharp, pointy knife for cutting casings and poking air pockets works well. Have on hand plenty of metal trays for spreading out the meats and holding the finished sausages. An ounce scale for measuring salt and a pound scale for measuring meat are invaluable. Have also metal mixing bowls, measuring spoons, cutting boards and spatulas, and an electric spice or coffee grinder for grinding spices. A little 3-pronged sausage pricker is handy for poking air holes, too.

Smoker

For making smoked sausages, a smoker is a necessity. A small electric smoker will work well, as will a freestanding smokehouse the size of a small apartment—get a smoker that suits your needs. We use a little electric smoker that maintains a temperature of around 225°F. This works great for most sausages, and for general smoking, too.

SUPPLIES

Salt

All measurements in this chapter are for kosher salt, and they are by weight. We use 1.25 ounces of salt for every 5 pounds of meat for fresh sausages (1.5 ounces for cured sausages), but please adjust this to suit your own taste.

Casings

We use natural hog casings, in several sizes: 29-mm casings will produce thinner links that grill quickly and make for good sandwiches, whereas the 32-mm and larger casings are good for smoking and stewing with beans. Casings can be ordered online and kept for a long time—they are preserved in salt; simply soak them in water for 30 minutes to remove the salt.

Spices

Good spices make a good sausage. Use fresh spices and grind them right before using them. We use a designated coffee grinder for this and it works great. A mortar and pestle also works wonderfully.

Fat

Game meats are almost completely lean, so fat must be added to make a palatable sausage. Sausages need to have at least 20 to 25 percent fat to have a nice texture and flavor. If you would like to use less fat in your sausages, we would recommend *not making sausages*. Use pork back fat, or "fatback," for adding to the sausage, though good quality beef fat can also be added. Do not use the softer "leaf" fat from the pig— this is for rendering into lard and tends to melt in sausages, resulting in a crumbly, mealy, dry texture. Adding pure fat allows the flavor of the game meat to shine, while minimizing filler meats. If fatback is not available, you can use a very fatty cut of pork, like belly, though you'll have to use a higher ratio of pork to game. When using fatback, use (for a 5-pound batch) a ratio of 1 or 1.25 pounds of fatback to 4 or 3.75 pounds of game meats, or 20 or 25 percent fat, respectively.

If using pork belly, which is approximately 50 percent fat, you would need to use a ratio of 1:1 pork belly to game, resulting in a mix that is 25 percent fat. Pork shoulder, which has a 25- to 30- percent fat content, won't provide enough fat for the finished game sausage. Try your hardest to find a source for good-quality pastured pork fat that has the same quality as your game meats rather than diluting free-ranging venison with cheap, factory-farmed pork.

1. Toss the weighed-out meats and fat with the spice mixture so that everything is nicely distributed.

2. Grind the meats and fats through the grinder into a metal tray. Place this try in the freezer or refrigerator if grinding a second time.

3. Mix the sausage in a stand mixer fitted with a paddle attachment, adding in cold liquid as called for in the recipe. This cold liquid helps bind the sausage together and disperses the seasonings evenly.

4

5

4. Mix until the ground meat, fat, and spices are well combined and the texture is tacky, about 1 to 3 minutes.

5. Place the sausage in the hopper of the sausage stuffer, pressing it down to remove air pockets. Thread a good amount of casing onto the stuffing tube, lubricating the tube with cold water so the casings will come off easily. Leave about 6 inches of casing at the end of the stuffing tube and tie a knot in this to prevent the sausage from coming out the end.

6. Then poke a small hole to allow air to escape.

6

7

8

9

7. Stuff the sausage into the casing, taking care not to overfill. You should be able to safely pinch the casing all the way without bursting it. Also, do not underfill, or the casing will shrink when cooked and be a little chewy.

8. Stuff the casing until you have a good, workable length of sausage in front of you. Form the links: pinch the casing at about 6 inches (or your desired link length) from the end, forming the first link. Pinch the casing again 6 inches from the first link and flip or turn away from you 6 to 8 times, forming two links. Pinch at the next 6 inches and the next, then twist the links 6 to 8 times toward you, forming the third and fourth links. Alternating the twists keeps the coil from unraveling. Repeat with the entire coil.

9. The finished sausages. Either hang the linked sausages in the refrigerator or spread them out on a tray lined with parchment paper for at least a day, preferably two, to allow the twists to dry and the sausages to firm up and develop flavor. After a couple of days, the sausages can be cut with scissors into links and either smoked, grilled, or packaged for later use.

Venison Breakfast Sausage

Sweet, peppery, and aggressively spiced, this patty sausage is great with eggs, a stack of pancakes, French toast, or used as a stuffing (Teal in a Jar, page 215) in savory dishes. This sausage is slightly leaner than the others, but feel free to increase the amount of pork fat in the recipe to 1½ pounds if you like.

2 tablespoons black peppercorns

1 tablespoon rubbed sage

2 teaspoons ground ginger or finely chopped fresh ginger

1 teaspoon cayenne pepper

¼ teaspoon ground nutmeg

4 pounds venison trim, cut into 2-inch pieces

1 pound pork fatback, cut into 2-inch pieces

1¼ ounces kosher salt

½ cup maple syrup

Makes 5 pounds

1. In a spice grinder or mortar, grind the black pepper, sage, ginger (if dried), cayenne, and nutmeg to a fine powder.

2. Mix together the venison, fatback, ground spices, ginger (if using fresh), and salt. Spread out on a baking sheet and freeze for 30 minutes.

3. Grind the meat through the medium plate of a meat grinder into a chilled bowl, then spread out on baking sheet and freeze for 10 minutes.

4. Grind the meat again through the medium plate into a chilled bowl. Add the maple syrup and mix well. Cook a small patty of the sausage, taste, and adjust the seasonings in the mixture.

5. Divide the sausage into 4 or 5 portions, wrap in plastic wrap, and refrigerate for up to 7 days or freeze for up to 6 months. To cook, form small, flat patties and brown on a griddle over medium-high heat.

Wild Boar Chorizo

Possibly my favorite breakfast is wild boar chorizo, eggs, and tortillas. The tangy, spicy chorizo goes well with so many things that I've even made whole feral pigs into just chorizo, after taking the chops off, of course. It's that good. Vary the cayenne and paprika used for more depth, or more or less heat.

1 tablespoon black peppercorns

1 tablespoon cumin seed

1 tablespoon dried oregano

1 tablespoon cayenne pepper

1 tablespoon smoked paprika

¼ teaspoon ground cinnamon

5 pounds fatty feral hog meat, or 4 pounds lean feral hog trim and 1 pound pork fatback, cut into 2-inch pieces

1¼ ounces kosher salt

¼ cup apple cider vinegar

Makes 5 pounds

1. In a spice grinder or mortar, grind the black pepper, cumin, oregano, cayenne, paprika, and cinnamon to a fine powder.

2. Mix together the pork, fatback, ground spices, and salt. Spread out on a baking sheet and freeze for 30 minutes.

3. Grind the meat through the medium plate of a meat grinder into a chilled bowl; spread out again on baking sheet and freeze for 10 minutes.

4. Grind again through the medium plate into a chilled bowl. Add the vinegar and mix well.

5. Cook a small patty of the chorizo, taste, and adjust the seasonings in the mixture. The chorizo will keep refrigerated for 7 days or in the freezer for up to 6 months. To cook, panfry the chorizo in a little oil over medium-low heat.

Wild Boar and Dark Beer Sausage

Dark beer really pops in this sausage because of the complementary molasses, spices, and mustard seed, but still lets the flavor of the feral hog come through. I like these in 6-inch links for serving on a roll or with some mashed potatoes and cabbage.

1 tablespoon black peppercorns

2 teaspoons ground ginger

2 teaspoons dried marjoram

½ teaspoon ground nutmeg

1 whole clove

1 dried bay leaf

5 pounds fatty wild boar trim, or 3½ pounds lean trim and 1½ pounds pork fatback, cut into 2-inch pieces

1¼ ounces kosher salt

2 tablespoons chopped garlic

1 tablespoon molasses

1 tablespoon whole yellow mustard seed

1 cup ice-cold dark beer

Hog casings, soaked for 30 minutes in cold water

Makes 5 pounds

1. In a spice grinder or mortar, grind the black pepper, ginger, marjoram, nutmeg, clove, and bay leaf to a fine powder.

2. Mix together the boar trim and fatback, ground spices, salt, garlic, molasses, and whole mustard seed. Spread out on a baking sheet and freeze for 30 minutes.

3. Grind the meat through the medium plate of a meat grinder into a chilled bowl; spread out again on baking sheet and freeze for 10 minutes.

4. Grind again through the medium plate of the grinder into a chilled bowl. In a stand mixer with a paddle attachment, mix the ground meat for one minute on medium speed, then slowly add the ice-cold beer, mixing for 1 minute more or until tacky.

5. Cook a small patty of the sausage, taste, and adjust the seasonings in the mixture, if needed.

6. Stuff the mixture into hog casings and twist into 6-inch links (see page 139). The sausages will keep refrigerated for 7 days or in the freezer for up to 6 months. To cook, panfry in a little oil over medium-low heat.

Venison Chaurice

The copious raw onions in this sausage, along with the classic Creole seasonings of allspice, bay, and cayenne, make this fresh sausage link perfectly adaptable to venison. Try this on the grill or smoked, or in dishes like rice pilafs, beans, and gumbos.

10 whole allspice berries

2 dried bay leaves

1 tablespoon black peppercorns

1 tablespoon cayenne pepper

1 teaspoon dried thyme

1 teaspoon dried oregano

3¾ pounds venison trim, cut into 2-inch pieces

1¼ pounds pork fatback, cut into 2-inch pieces

1¼ ounces kosher salt

2 onions, chopped

1 cup ice-cold water

Hog casings, soaked for 30 minutes in cold water

Makes 5 pounds

1. In a spice grinder or mortar, grind the allspice, bay leaves, black pepper, cayenne, thyme, and oregano to a fine powder.

2. Mix the venison, fatback, ground spices, salt, and onions. Spread out on a baking sheet and freeze for 30 minutes.

3. Grind the meat through the medium plate of a meat grinder into a chilled bowl, then spread out again on the baking sheet and freeze for 10 minutes.

4. In a stand mixer with a paddle attachment, mix the ground meat for 30 seconds on medium speed; then slowly add the ice-cold water, mix for 1 minute more, or until tacky.

5. Cook a small patty of the sausage, taste, and adjust the seasonings in the mixture. Stuff the mixture into hog casings and twist into 6-inch links (see page 139). The chaurice will keep refrigerated for 7 days or in the freezer for up to 6 months. Cook the chaurice on the grill or in a smoker.

Smoked Goose Sausage

This sausage conveys the flavor of the bird with smoke, salt, and spices, and is a great use for a bounty of goose. Serve this with buttered cabbage and mashed potatoes, on a roll with sauerkraut, or sliced cold with mustard. Links of smoked goose sausage served with Goose Leg Confit (page 220) would be fitting, too.

1 teaspoon caraway seed

1 teaspoon coriander seed

1 teaspoon granulated garlic

10 whole juniper berries

¼ teaspoon ground nutmeg

1 tablespoon whole black peppercorns

3¾ pounds goose breast and leg, trimmed of most sinew

1¼ pounds pork fatback

1¼ ounces kosher salt

¾ teaspoon Insta Cure No. 1*

2 tablespoons brown sugar

¼ cup nonfat dry milk powder

½ cup ice-cold water

Hog casings, soaked for 30 minutes in cold water

Makes 5 pounds

1. In a spice grinder or mortar, grind the caraway, coriander, garlic, juniper, and nutmeg to a powder. Add the peppercorns to the grinder and pulse to just crush them.

2. Cut the goose and fatback into large cubes and put in the freezer until just frozen. Add the ground spices, salt, Insta Cure, and brown sugar and mix well. Grind the meat through the medium plate of a meat grinder into a chilled bowl. Spread out on a baking sheet and freeze for 20 minutes.

3. Grind again through the medium plate of the grinder and put in the chilled bowl of a stand mixer with a paddle attachment. Mix the sausage for about 30 seconds on low speed; then add the nonfat dry milk powder. Mix for another 30 seconds, add the ice water, and mix for 1 minute more, or until tacky.

4. Cook a small patty of the sausage, taste, and adjust the seasonings in the mixture, if needed. Stuff the mixture into hog casings and twist into 6-inch links (see page 139). Hang the links, uncovered, in the refrigerator for 2 to 3 days, or until the outsides are very dry.

5. Heat a smoker to 225°F. Smoke the sausages for 30 to 45 minutes, or until the internal temperature registers 155°F. Remove the sausages and refrigerate them immediately. The sausages will keep refrigerated for 7 days or in the freezer for up 6 months. To serve, slice and serve cold with mustard, or reheat on a hot grill and serve with mustard and sauerkraut.

*Curing salt necessary to inhibit growth of bacteria. Use and store with caution.

Dry-Cured Sausage

Vary the flavors of this dry-cured sausage* by adding different herbs, more garlic, citrus zest, fennel seed, hot pepper, etc. The key is to use exact amounts of salt and curing salt, then allow it to dry in a semi-humid area such as a wine cellar or a designated curing fridge. This sausage can be also be cured in a standard fridge, but may take on some of the refrigerator odors, and will take longer at the lower temperature.

4 pounds wild boar or venison trim,
   cut into cubes

1 teaspoon Insta Cure No. 2**

1½ ounces kosher salt

6 garlic cloves, finely chopped

4 teaspoons coarse black pepper

½ teaspoon dried thyme

1 pound pork fatback, finely diced

¼ cup very cold red wine

Hog casings, soaked for 30 minutes
   in cold water

Makes 3½ pounds

1. Mix the boar thoroughly with the Insta Cure, salt, garlic, pepper, and thyme and grind through the medium plate of a meat grinder. Spread out on a baking sheet and freeze for 20 minutes.

2. In a stand mixer with a paddle attachment, mix the ground meat with the fatback for 1 minute on medium speed, slowly add the red wine, and mix about 1 minute more, or until tacky.

3. Cook a small patty of the sausage, taste, and adjust the seasonings in the mixture, if needed. Stuff the mixture into the casings, making 16-inch loops, and tie the two ends together with string.

4. Hang the sausages at 60°F with 60-percent humidity until firm and dry, 4 to 5 weeks. Mold may form on the outside of the sausage. Fuzzy or greenish mold is bad. Throw out your sausage if this develops. If it smells off, or if it is mushy or not dried through, do not eat it. At the conclusion of the drying phase, the sausage is ready to serve or can be wrapped and refrigerated for up to 4 months.

*Dry-curing is a temperamental process, dependent on air and humidity, and involves safety and sanitation issues that may deter novices. Safety is important: you can make yourself or someone else very sick with improperly cured meats.

**Curing salt necessary to inhibit growth of bacteria. Use and store with caution.

SAUSAGE & CHARCUTERIE

Deer & Turkey

TARGETS OF OPPORTUNITY

The wind wouldn't seem so intense if we weren't sitting in a metal box fifteen feet above the ground. Due north is at my left elbow, and the wind is coursing through the box blind that sits over a dirt road in the Texas Hill Country. This spot is the back forty of a farm—a very nice farm that I buy a lot of vegetables from. It is, to my knowledge, never hunted.

The dusty white road runs from left to right in the bottom of a narrow valley, flanked on either side by thick juniper, with taller oaks dotting the hillsides on three sides. Luckily, the blind sits on a site well traveled by game, and there's a pond a hundred yards away.

Today, we are seeking a deer or a turkey, whichever shows itself first. Both inhabit the property in good numbers and both are delicious, so we decide not to confine ourselves to any objective other than targets of opportunity. The wind is ripping, making the animals wary; their senses of smell (deer) and hearing (deer and turkeys) are affected by the swirling canyon currents, swaying limbs, and creaking branches. I have that unsettled feeling we're not going to see any action this morning.

On the pre-dawn drive in, deer were everywhere, finishing their errands in the last light of a waning full moon. Now we sit in the blind, resigned to an uneventful and blustery day. Then, like a clap of thunder, comes a series of gobbles and yelps from turkeys descending their roost to our north, over the next rocky ridge. We wait, hoping they'll head this way. Thirty minutes tick by and nothing.

Then, another round of yelps. It sounds like a few hens are a couple hundred yards to the north where we expected them. We peer past the big cedar branches that are slowly engulfing the blind and look toward the pond, but see nothing. Something catches my eye directly below us on the road, and before I know it, a

I grab my backpack and rifle and carefully descend the cold metal ladder from the blind, elated by my luck and happy with my reaction. Walking up on the second bird, I see that it is a big bird, indeed, with the long beard and big spurs of a mature turkey. The first bird, lying five feet from where I shot it, could be its twin. Picking both up at the same time is a strain, and causes me to reflect on the sheer majesty of these birds. Turkeys have incredible eyesight, can soar beautifully across canyons, and are just gorgeous birds to look at. Their size is grand, too, providing a lot of delectable material for my freezer. Times two.

We stash the birds in the best place we can find— the backseat of an abandoned Suburban at the base of the steep hill to the east—and plan the rest of the morning. Since it is already an unqualified success, I suggest a hike to the top of the hill—the tallest for miles, overlooking a beautiful river valley—to see if anything is moving in the flat meadow at its peak. We make the steep fifteen-minute hike, pausing halfway to watch the sun begin to cast long shadows over the valley behind us and have a water break. As we near the top, I slow down, take a minute to catch my breath, and carefully peer over the embankment at the end of the long meadow.

A road runs around the perimeter of this mesa-type hill, with the ubiquitous stands of juniper and twisting oaks dotted with spiny agarita and calf-high clumps of prairie grasses. We hug the inside of the road to the left, walking straight into the still-lashing north wind. I have often seen deer up on the top here, eating grass and then slowly filtering down the hill to bedding areas. Walking very slowly, I am watching ahead, banking on the wind to cover my movements and scent, but not fully expecting to see anything.

group of six large toms is slowly and steadily cruising by, at a distance of about fifteen yards. I shoulder the rifle, flip off the safety, and aim at a clear patch in the dense brush below. A turkey passes by quickly, then another, and another. A big gobbler enters the five-foot clearing and I fire, aiming high and back to preserve the breast. The shot shatters the stillness like it always does, and I see the bird flop as I swing the rifle to my right, chambering a second round, hoping they run into the clearing to our right, which they do.

Another big tom runs up a steep embankment and pauses, perhaps confused by the wind. I fire again and he drops heavily. I chamber another round, fire at a third tom running straight toward us, and miss, kicking up a cloud of caliche on the road behind him.

Knowing they'll be gone by the time I can reload, I don't even bother. Not to mention I already have two

A flicker of a tail dead in front of me immediately says deer. I freeze, then look to my left. In another cosmic testament to the great luck I am having this morning, the closest tree to me, a young oak, has a perfect fork in its main trunk, right about shoulder height. Not only this, but there is a large, perfectly flat rock at its base that, when I stand on it, puts me at an optimal height to use the tree as a gun rest. I find the deer in my binoculars and try to assess its size. Hill Country deer can be tiny sometimes, and I don't want to shoot a yearling. The deer is obscured by trees and facing toward me, so I can't yet discern whether it's a shooter or not. The flicking tail tells me that she's seen movement in my direction and is expressing some concern. I put the scope on her, waiting for her to move, when a larger shape catches my eye. At first I think it's a tree, but then it moves . . . a bigger deer.

The buck moves to my left at a pace that suggests

he's spooked, and then he's just gone. I pan right, to where I saw the doe earlier, and see nothing. Damn. Then I sight a deer shape, again standing behind a tree facing me. Soon, she emerges, looking right at me, and she's of good size—not big, but nice. I imagine what this looks like to her—can she see a reflection off of the scope? I am mostly obscured by the tree and am not moving a muscle. She stares for what feels like a long half-minute, then turns. I almost take the shot, but she is still quartering toward me at a bad angle and is about 120 yards away. She walks behind another tree and pauses, flicking that big white tail all the while. I know that I have no time to waste here—she is getting more agitated by the second and I have to take the first good shot. She moves away from the tree, still quartering toward me, when I aim for the middle of her right shoulder and fire. She drops immediately and then I make a mistake; I look away

for a second. When I look back, she's gone, but I see a shadow of movement to the left of where I hit her, which would be the logical escape route, following that buck.

I stop and get the binoculars out. Scanning the shade underneath the trees close to her last position, I see white belly, but then realize it's just a chunk of limestone like the one I'm standing on. I know I made a good shot, but this is always the moment that is hardest with hunting larger animals. Is it down? Will I be able to track it?

Not wanting to push the doe should she be wounded, I go ahead about fifty yards to get a better vantage point and again scan the ground. Another rock imposter fools me for a second, then I see legs. She is down, and is lying less than twenty feet from where I shot her.

Walking up on the pretty doe, I feel the same sadness and happiness that I feel every time: elation on finding her, the tangible discomfort of taking the life of an animal, the pride and comfort of having the nourishment from her, and the anticipation of the next part of the job—converting this deer lying in a grass meadow on top of a hill into an array of edibles.

The Gambrel Method

This method is for the times when you are able to hang a deer (or hog) from gambrels (a large, sturdy, coathanger-shaped device that presents the deer at a comfortable working level and spreads the legs apart for easy cleaning). Suspend your gambrels from a strong tree limb or over a thick beam in a shed. Having someone to help hoist the deer up and hold it steady is great, too.

    Clean hogs the same way, but know that their skin requires more work to get it off. Typically, you'll have to cut against the skin constantly, pulling downward to free the bristly hide from the body. Take your time with a hog and try to leave as much of the fat as possible on the carcass. I like to use a hooked skinning knife—the hooked blade catches the skin and unzips it easily, and prevents unintentional nicking of intestines, which you don't want. If you do accidentally cut into an intestine or stomach—and you'll know when you do—don't despair. Just work quickly to get the guts out, keeping the intestines away from the meat as best you can, then rinse the carcass very well. Animals that have been gut shot or have some internal organ damage should be dressed in the field (see Field Dressing, page 102) as soon as possible to prevent contamination.

Tools needed: two knives (we recommend a hooked skinning knife and a boning knife, or just a good, sharp pocketknife), bone saw or lopping shears, gut bucket, garbage bags, plastic gloves (optional) and gallon freezer bags for the offal

1. Carefully make a cut parallel to the leg between the tendon and the bone. Do not cut through the tendon.

2. With a sharp, thin-bladed knife, carefully cut around the anus, as if coring an apple. Once partially cut, pull the intestine out a little and carefully continue cutting around the intestine until it is free.

1

2

3

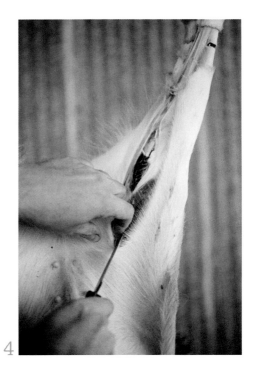

4

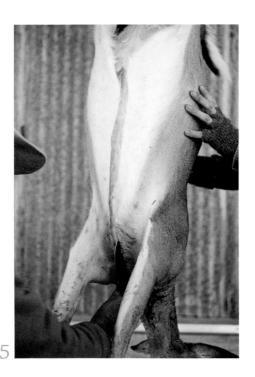

5

3. Hang the deer from the gambrels with the head down, belly facing you. Without severing the leg tendons, cut just through the skin at the "knee" joint, all the way around the legs in preparation for skinning.

4. If cleaning a male animal, cut under the penis from the front side, lifting carefully and cutting the urinary tract away from the body. Once fully trimmed away, hang the penis and urinary tract over the back side of the deer. Using the hooked skinning knife or a sharp knife, cut from the "knee" down to the abdomen on both sides, meeting in the middle.

5. Cut from this juncture through the skin down the center of the deer all the way to the throat, taking great care not to puncture the intestines.

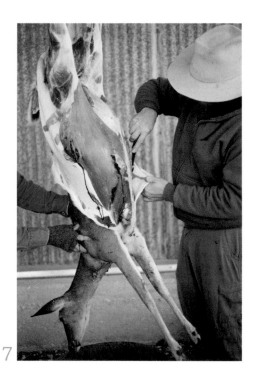

6. Cut through the skin of the front legs down to the knees, then cut all the way around the legs.

7. Begin skinning the deer from the top down, using a sharp knife and applying pressure against the skin in gentle, sweeping motions. Try to leave as little meat as possible on the skin.

8. Cut through the tail at its base with the broad base of a knife.

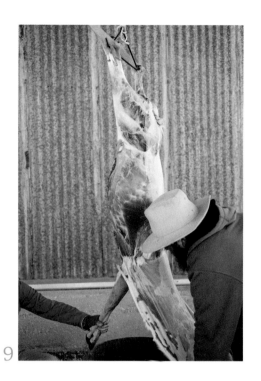

9

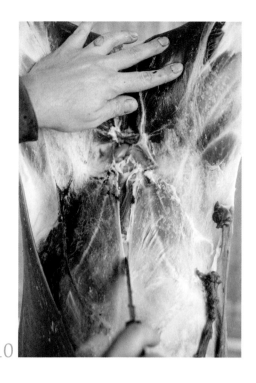

10

11

9. Once the deer is skinned about halfway down, roll the skin up and grip it very firmly, then pull downward, pulling the skin off of the deer. Trim with a knife as necessary to remove all of the skin. Cut the head off right below the jawbone with the lopping shears, and by twisting the head forcefully. Depending on local regulations, the head may need to accompany the deer to its final destination. If saving the hide for tanning, either freeze now or salt the skin side very heavily and roll up.

10. Cut all the way down to the pelvic bone, and make slight incisions on either side just below the pelvic bone to begin gutting. With the hooked knife or with a thin blade facing out, begin making an incision from the pelvic bone all the way down to the sternum. The offal will begin to fall off.

11. Once you reach the ribs, use a sturdy knife to cut through the sternum all the way to the neck.

12

13

12. Place a large bucket or other receptacle under the deer and gently pull the intestine through the area under the pelvis. Begin pulling the guts out of the deer with firm downward pressure. The cored-out intestine should come with the mass of viscera—if it does not, cut the connecting tissue so that it is freed. Pull the spongy lungs and heart from the deer, then grip the tubelike trachea and get as much out as possible, pulling upward.

13. From the viscera, remove the heart and liver, if desired; set aside in plastic bags. If possible, rinse the deer well with cold water, or spray it with a 1:1 solution of distilled vinegar and water to retard spoilage.

14. Cut off the legs at the joints with the lopping shears or saw.

14

Storing Large Game Before Processing

There are a lot of methods and opinions on this, and this is ours: cold and dry. The optimal, but unlikely, method is to hang the skinned and gutted deer in a walk-in cooler (below 40°F) for a couple of days or up to a week, depending on the age of the deer (longer for older animals). If storing in a cooler, wrap the deer very well in plastic garbage bags, then put it on a layer of ice. Add as much ice as the cooler will hold. Remove the drain plug to keep water from pooling, and add more ice as outside temperatures dictate. If cold overnight (or daytime) temperatures are present, hang the deer outside; a cold, breezy night is perfect, but low freezing temperatures will do that—freeze your deer. Don't hang a deer outside if it's above 40°F or below, say, 25°F, though hanging the deer in a cold shed or garage during low temperatures is great.

A word on "wet aging" . . . It is, in our opinion, vastly better to keep meats dry and cold. Popular methods for storing game include covering them directly with ice to ostensibly remove gamey flavor and cool them, but we feel this is counterproductive. Contact with water actually leaches out moisture, making meats soggy on the outside and eventually drier when cooked. When aged in a dry environment, meat develops a dry, almost hard exterior that seals in the moisture naturally found in muscle tissues, resulting in a better texture and flavor. Game—especially hogs—shouldn't need to be soaked in ice water, and we've found that when dry aged, even large boars have a great flavor if cooled quickly and cooked properly. Hang hogs for 1 to 5 days before butchering.

Butchering a Deer

The following is exactly how I cut deer for consumption in my home. It yields a good mix of cuts for grilling, braising, stock, sausage, ground meat, and more. Follow Butchering a Feral Hog (page 108) to yield chops and saddles from your deer, if you prefer.*

1

Tools needed: a boning knife, bone saw, cleaver (optional), and rubber mallet (optional)

1. Remove the tenderloins from the inside of the intestinal cavity. These are the two small, thin, tapered muscles running along the underside of the backbone to the back legs.

2. Trim the tenderloins of most of the attached fat and silverskin, and set aside for tartare (page 169) or for grilling over a very hot fire to medium rare.

3. Cut above the back legs with the knife to the bone. Cut through the bone with the saw. Set the back legs aside.

4. Cut all four shanks off above the joint, and set aside for Onion Soup (page 177) and Venison Barbacoa (page 168).

5. Make a cut between the third and fourth ribs from the neck, using the knife to cut all the way to the bone. Always cut through flesh with a knife, and bone with a saw or cleaver. Cut the shoulders off with a saw. A small, round part of the shoulder blade will remain in the middle section; cut this out and use it for stock.

6. Cut the neck into 3- or 4-inch pieces for Venison Neck Osso Buco (page 170) or Venison Barbacoa (page 168). Bone the shoulder out for sausages (page 140) or Venison Burgers (page 180).

*Please note that in areas where Chronic Wasting Disease is present, there may be some risk in using or cutting venison bones and spinal tissue. Check with your local Department of Natural Resources or your state's wildlife managing authority for information and current warnings about CWD.

2

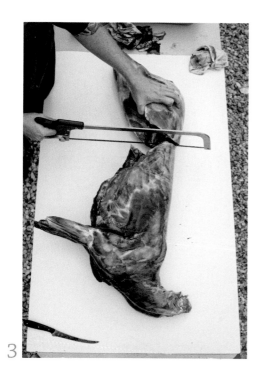

3

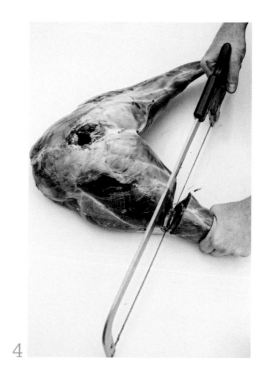

4

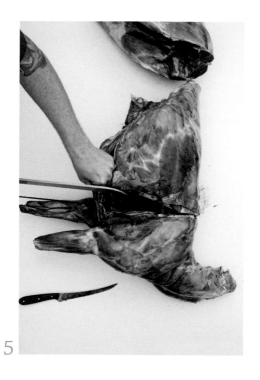

5

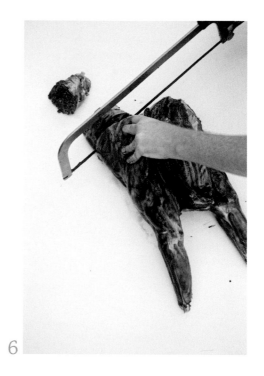

6

7

8

7. Remove the flanks. Find the loin muscles (backstraps) and make a cut beneath them from front to back. Carefully cut the meat away from the ribs, holding the flanks in one hand and gently and slowly working the knife against the rib bones until you have a large, rectangular piece. Set this aside for Stuffed Venison Flank (page 166).

8. Remove the loins by cutting against the spine, then downward and outward to the ribs. Peel the silverskin from the loins, and set any scrap aside for grinding. Set the rib cage aside for stock (page 173).

9. The loins.

9

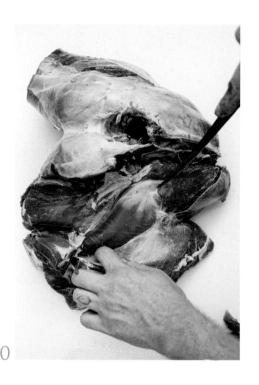

10

11

12

10. Following the natural seams of the leg muscles, carefully work around each muscle, using a combination of cutting and pulling.

11. Once each muscle is freed, set aside and trim of all silverskin.

12. Use the leg muscles for Venison Bresaola (page 128) or substitute for Turkey Cutlets (page 191), or bone out the legs entirely and ground for sausage. Save the leg bones for stock (page 173).

Stuffed Venison Flank

The flank—a misunderstood throwaway cut—can be transformed through long, slow cooking. Stuffing this sinewy, tough cut with fatty sausage keeps it moist, while the bread crumbs and egg set the stuffing and make it sliceable. Try this recipe with different sausages in the stuffing—we've had success with wild boar chorizo, kielbasa, and a simple garlic sausage. The acid from the tomatoes and wine tenderizes the braise, creating a rich sauce that calls for mashed potatoes, polenta, or pasta. Try making this a day ahead and reheating it slowly.

1 boneless venison flank, about 2 to 3 pounds, (page 164)

Kosher salt and freshly ground black pepper

1 pound ground pork or sausage

2 tablespoons chopped fresh sage or parsley

1 cup fresh bread crumbs

2 eggs, beaten

4 tablespoons olive oil

2 onions, thinly sliced

2 cups carrots, thickly sliced

4 garlic cloves, sliced

One 28-ounce can crushed tomatoes

1 cup red or white wine

Venison stock (page 173), chicken stock, or water, as needed

½ cup chopped fresh parsley

Serves 8

1. Preheat the oven to 350°F. Season the flank with salt and pepper.

2. In a small bowl, mix the ground pork, sage, bread crumbs, and eggs. Season with salt and pepper; omit the seasoning if using bulk sausage.

3. Lay the flank in front of you with the grain running across, from side to side. Spread the pork mixture across the center of the flank, roll the flank around the stuffing, then tie with kitchen twine every 2 inches.

4. In a large Dutch oven or braising pot, heat the olive oil over medium-high heat and brown the stuffed flank on all sides, about 15 minutes total. Transfer the flank to a plate.

5. Add the onions, carrots, and garlic to the pan and cook over medium-high heat until softened, about 5 minutes. Add the tomatoes and wine and cook until reduced by half, about 10 minutes. Return the flank to the pot, spoon some sauce over it, and add enough stock or water to cover the meat halfway.

6. Cover the pot, bring to a boil, then place the pot in the oven. Braise, turning the flank every 30 minutes, until tender, 4 to 5 hours, adding more stock, if necessary, to keep the flank half covered.

7. Taste the finished sauce and adjust seasoning with salt and pepper. Let the flank rest for 5 minutes, cut away the twine, and slice thickly against the grain. Garnish with the chopped parsley.

Venison Barbacoa

Shredded, tender shards of spiced venison make a perfect breakfast on tortillas. Substitute any large game for the venison, like aoudad, feral hogs, elk, or even duck, turkey, or goose legs. Slow cookers are perfect for preparations like this; put it on at night and a hearty breakfast is ready the next morning.

2½ pounds venison trim, shanks and necks*

2 tablespoons apple cider vinegar

2 tablespoons lime juice

2 dried chipotle chiles

1 onion, chopped

2 teaspoons ground cumin

2 teaspoons Mexican oregano

2 teaspoons kosher salt

1 teaspoon freshly ground black pepper

2 whole cloves, ground

2 dried bay leaves, ground

⅛ teaspoon ground cinnamon

Serves 4

1. Combine all of the ingredients in a slow cooker and cover with cold water by about 2 inches. Cook on low for 6 to 8 hours until very tender.

2. Remove the meat from the pot and cool slightly, reserving the liquid. Shred the meat, removing the bones, and moisten the meat with a few ladles of the reserved broth.

3. Adjust the seasoning and serve with tortillas, chopped raw onion, cilantro, limes, salsa, and a vinegary hot sauce.

*Please note that in areas where Chronic Wasting Disease is present, there may be some risk in using or cutting venison bones and spinal tissue. Check with your local Department of Natural Resources or your state's wildlife managing authority for information and current warnings about CWD.

Venison Tartare

Perhaps the best way to enjoy fresh-killed venison or antelope: raw. If you are concerned about ingesting raw meat, freeze the venison for a couple of weeks first. (There is also a risk in consuming raw eggs, so use one from a reputable source.) I strongly recommend trying this dish, as it is a distillation of venison flavor.

1 pound venison tenderloin or loin (backstrap), trimmed of any sinew

Kosher salt and freshly ground black pepper

6 dashes Worcestershire sauce

6 dashes Tabasco sauce

1 tablespoon coarse ground mustard

Zest of 1 lemon

¼ cup chopped fresh parsley or arugula

2 tablespoons finely chopped red onion or shallot

1 very fresh farm egg yolk

Coarse sea salt, for garnish

Serves 4

1. Finely dice the venison. With a heavy, very sharp knife, chop the meat to a fine consistency, but not a paste.

2. In a large bowl, mix the venison with the remaining ingredients, adjusting as needed. Refrigerate for up to 1 hour.

3. Mold the tartare into a bowl or ramekin and invert onto a plate. Sprinkle coarse salt on top. Serve cold with grilled bread and a green salad, or with french fries.

Venison Neck Osso Buco

The classic Italian braise of veal shanks is most noteworthy for its ingenious use of gremolata —finely chopped garlic, parsley, and lemon— which complements the savory meat and adds acidity and interest. This recipe uses venison neck, which also has a hole (buco) in the bone (osso), and benefits from long, slow cooking. I prefer the flavor of white wine in osso buco, but use red wine if you like.

4 cuts venison neck,* about 3 to 4 inches, or substitute venison or wild boar shanks

Kosher salt and freshly ground black pepper

1 cup all-purpose flour (optional)

4 tablespoons olive oil

2 large onions, sliced

4 carrots, sliced

1 celery stalk, sliced (optional)

6 fresh sage leaves

2 bay leaves

1 cup white wine

1 quart Venison Stock (page 173), **chicken stock, or water**

Zest of 1 lemon

½ cup chopped fresh parsley

6 to 10 garlic cloves, finely chopped

Serves 4

1. Preheat the oven to 300°F.

2. Season the venison necks with salt and pepper. Dredge the necks in the flour, if using.

3. Heat the olive oil in a large Dutch oven or heavy-bottomed pot over medium-high heat and brown the necks well. Transfer the necks to a plate, lower the heat to medium, and add the onions, carrots, celery, if using, sage, and bay leaves. Cook, stirring often, until tender, about 10 minutes. Add the wine, necks, and enough stock to cover by 2 inches and bring to a simmer.

4. Cover the pot and place in the oven. Cook the venison until it is very tender, about 4 hours. (Alternatively, the ingredients can be cooked in a slow cooker on low heat until tender, 4 to 6 hours.) Transfer the necks to a serving platter and reduce the sauce over high heat on the stove until it is slightly thickened, 5 to 10 minutes, then season with salt and pepper.

5. To make the gremolata, chop the lemon zest, parsley, and garlic together until very fine. Just before serving, stir half of the gremolata into the sauce, and then pour the sauce over the necks. Sprinkle the remaining gremolata over the top. This dish goes very well with mashed potatoes or the traditional saffron risotto.

*Please note that in areas where Chronic Wasting Disease is present, there may be some risk in using or cutting venison bones and spinal tissue. Check with your local Department of Natural Resources or your state's wildlife managing authority for information and current warnings about CWD.

Venison Chili

Without getting into any heated debates about chili ingredients and so forth, this recipe is a good start—feel free to add spices, garlic, and even beans, if you must. Playing with different hot pepper powders will yield different levels of heat and flavor. We use a mix of ground and venison trim for texture and added body, and the optional shank adds even more. Wild boar is a good stand-in for the venison or may be used in combination.

This recipe makes a lot of chili; leftovers will freeze very well and make a perfect winter meal with cornbread, chopped raw onion, cheddar cheese, and some pickled jalapeños.

¼ cup bacon fat or lard

5 pounds ground venison

5 pounds venison trim, cut into 2-inch pieces

10 onions, chopped

¼ cup kosher salt

2 tablespoons freshly ground black pepper

2 tablespoons ground cumin

2 tablespoons Mexican oregano

2 tablespoons chipotle chili powder

2 tablespoons sweet paprika

2 tablespoons ancho chili powder

1 tablespoon cayenne pepper

½ teaspoon ground cinnamon

4 cups canned crushed tomatoes

6 quarts Venison Stock (page 173), **chicken stock, or water**

1 venison shank or neck,* optional

Serves 12

*Please note that in areas where Chronic Wasting Disease is present, there may be some risk in using or cutting venison bones and spinal tissue. Check with your local Department of Natural Resources or your state's wildlife managing authority for information and current warnings about CWD.

1. Heat the fat in a large stockpot or Dutch oven over high heat and brown the meat very well, working in batches, if necessary. This browning process adds lots of flavor to the chili.

2. Add the onion and all of the spices to the meat and cook for a few minutes more. Add the tomatoes, stock, and optional shank, bring to a simmer, lower the heat, and cook until the stew meat is very, very tender, about 4 to 5 hours, stirring occasionally. Adjust salt and pepper to taste.

3. Remove the shank from the chili, let cool slightly, and shred the meat. Return the shredded meat back to the pot, stir, and serve.

Making Stock

There is satisfaction in knowing that you've used every bit of an animal you've hunted. It ends with stock. Through the simple act of cooking the bones with water, you render the bones useful by extracting nutrients from them. We make stock out of everything, from venison bones to feral hog bones to leftover dove carcasses—because stock is better than water and will give your braises, soups, and stews incredible—er—backbone and substance. Silverskin, scrap, and other bits also find their way into the stockpot, where they will break down into the gelatin and collagen that makes stock so good. Use fresh vegetables— or the skins and peelings from vegetables—too. Stock stores well, especially if reduced to a rich glaze, which can then be either rehydrated or used for dense sauces.

Venison or Feral Hog Stock

Venison or feral hog bones and scrap*

Onions, carrots, and celery

A few juniper berries, black peppercorns, and bay leaves

In a stockpot, cover all ingredients with cold water and bring to a simmer. Skim off any foam from the surface and continue to simmer at a gentle bubble—never a boil—for 6 to 10 hours, topping off with water as needed. Allow to cool slightly, then carefully strain the stock through a fine-mesh strainer or cheesecloth. The stock can now be cooled, packaged into pint or quart containers (leave headroom if freezing) or reduced. To reduce, put the stock in a clean pot and gently simmer until reduced by half or more. Package this concentrated stock as described above.

Game Bird Stock

Game bird bones

Onions and carrots

Black peppercorns and bay leaves

Game bird bones may be roasted for a richer, sweeter stock, or left unroasted. To roast, preheat the oven to 400°F. Lay the carcasses on a metal baking sheet and roast until browned, about 20 minutes. Place the roasted bones in a pot, and scrape any browned bits from the sheet into the pot, too, adding a bit of water and heat to loosen them if necessary. Add the vegetables to the pot, and then cover with cold water and bring to a simmer. Skim any foam, allowing the stock to cook for about 6 hours. Strain and package.

*Please note that in areas where Chronic Wasting Disease is present, there may be some risk in using or cutting venison bones and spinal tissue. Check with your local Department of Natural Resources or your state's wildlife managing authority for information and current warnings about CWD.

Venison Salpicon

This cold, shredded venison preparation is great on tostadas, eaten just with avocados—or add rice and beans and hard-boiled eggs for a traditional Salvadoran meal. Choose cuts of venison that will be tender and form long strands of cooked meat, like trimmings from the ribs, the breast (brisket), or the flank.

1 pound venison trimmings, breast, or flank

1 bay leaf

2 onions, 1 halved and 1 chopped finely

2 tablespoons olive oil

Juice of 1 large lime or 5 Key limes

½ teaspoon dried Mexican oregano

1 jalapeño pepper, seeded and finely chopped

2 small radishes, finely chopped

Kosher salt and freshly ground black pepper

About 12 fresh mint leaves, very thinly sliced

Serves 4 to 6

1. In a stockpot over high heat, combine the venison, bay leaf, halved onion, and enough water to cover, and bring to a simmer. Lower the heat and gently simmer until very tender, about 3 hours.

2. Remove the venison and let cool. Strain the stock, let cool, and refrigerate for another use.

3. In a bowl, combine the chopped onion, olive oil, lime juice, oregano, jalapeño, and radishes. Season with salt and pepper.

4. Shred the venison into small pieces and add to the bowl. Toss well, add the mint leaves, and adjust salt and pepper. Serve cold with warm rice and beans mixed together, hard-boiled egg, and chopped avocado.

Grilled Venison Loin with Horseradish Cream

According to our plan for deer (page 162), the loin, or "backstrap," is reserved for cooking whole, and tougher leg muscles are for pounding into cutlets. Here, the loin, the most tender part of the deer, is cooked rare to medium rare, preferably over a hot, smoky grill. Acidic crème fraîche or sour cream cuts the richness of the venison, and the horseradish adds quick heat.

1½ to 2 pounds venison loin, trimmed of all silverskin

Kosher salt and freshly ground black pepper

2 tablespoons finely chopped fresh herbs: thyme, marjoram, oregano, rosemary, savory, and/or parsley

3 tablespoons olive oil

1 cup crème fraîche or sour cream

2 tablespoons or more freshly grated or prepared horseradish

2 teaspoons chopped fresh chives or parsley

Juice and zest of 1 lemon

Serves 4

1. Season the meat with salt and pepper. In a small bowl, mix the 2 tablespoons herbs with the olive oil and spread all over the meat. Marinate for 2 hours or overnight, refrigerated.

2. Make a hot, even fire in a charcoal grill, or set a gas grill on high heat.

3. Grill the meat on one side without moving it until nicely browned, 4 to 5 minutes, then rotate 90 degrees to make grill marks and to char more surface area. Flip the loin, cooking 4 to 5 minutes more. Aim for a good, deeply browned char on the outside but leaving the meat still nice and rare on the inside. Transfer to a warm plate and allow to rest for at least 10 minutes while you prepare the sauce.

4. For the horseradish sauce, mix the crème fraîche, horseradish, chives, lemon juice, and zest together in a small bowl, and season with salt. Serve the loin, thinly sliced against the grain, with the horseradish cream, mashed potatoes, and a simple salad or green beans.

Onion Soup with Venison Shanks

This is a classic French onion soup with the addition of rich, long-cooked venison shanks. By cooking the oft-discarded skinny shanks of the venison in this way, you extract not only the rich stock from the bones, but utilize the scant but valuable meat from the legs. The long cooking process melds the sweetness of the copious onions and the meatiness of the venison, making this a perfect cold-weather dish. Use the best Gruyère you can get your hands on.

4 venison shanks* (about 4 pounds), cut into 6- to 8-inch pieces

Kosher salt and freshly ground black pepper

4 tablespoons olive oil

10 large onions, sliced

2 bay leaves

¼ cup sherry or balsamic vinegar

4 slices of good bread

4 thick slices of Gruyère or Emmentaler cheese

Serves 4

1. Season the venison shanks with salt and pepper. Heat the olive oil in a large Dutch oven or heavy-bottomed pot over medium-high heat and brown the shanks well, about 8 minutes.

2. Transfer the shanks to a plate, lower the heat to medium, add the onions and bay leaves, and cook, stirring often, until deeply browned and caramelized, about 30 minutes.

3. Add the sherry or balsamic vinegar, shanks, and enough water to cover by 4 inches, and bring to a simmer. Lower the heat and cook the venison until it is very tender, about 5 hours, adding more water, if necessary, to keep the shanks covered. Alternatively, the mixture can be cooked in a slow cooker on low heat for 4 to 6 hours, until tender.

4. Preheat the broiler. Lightly toast the bread. Cover each slice of toast with a slice of cheese, and broil until the cheese is melted, browned, and bubbling.

5. Season the soup with salt and lots of pepper, and then divide the shanks and soup among four large bowls. Place a piece of toast, covered with melted cheese, in each bowl and serve immediately with a simple salad and red wine.

*Please note that in areas where Chronic Wasting Disease is present, there may be some risk in using or cutting venison bones and spinal tissue. Check with your local Department of Natural Resources or your state's wildlife managing authority for information and current warnings about CWD.

Venison Moussaka

This is one of my favorite things to eat in the summer, when eggplants—my favorite vegetable, or at least in the top five—are at their peak. The unlikely combination of venison, roasted eggplant, béchamel, Parmesan, and lots of cinnamon is actually wonderful and surprisingly cohesive. I always serve this in the summer at room temperature with a salad of cucumbers, sweet peppers, tomatoes, basil, and onion, with a little vinegar, olive oil, and dried oregano. In the winter, serve it hot with a salad of lettuces in a sharp vinaigrette.

⅔ cup olive oil

2 pounds ground venison

Kosher salt and freshly ground black pepper

3 medium onions, chopped

6 garlic cloves, chopped

1 tablespoon dried oregano

4 tablespoons tomato paste

One 28-ounce can crushed tomatoes

1 cup chopped fresh parsley

4 medium eggplants, cut into ½-inch slices

8 tablespoons (1 stick) unsalted butter

¾ cup all-purpose flour

5 cups milk

8 egg yolks

2 teaspoons ground cinnamon

¾ teaspoon ground nutmeg

½ cup grated Parmesan cheese

Serves 8

1. Heat 3 tablespoons of the olive oil in a stockpot or Dutch oven over high heat and add the ground venison. Brown the venison very well, stirring occasionally, about 15 minutes. Lower the heat to medium, season with salt and pepper, and add the onions, garlic, oregano, and tomato paste. Cook until the onions are tender, stirring occasionally, about 10 minutes. Add the crushed tomatoes and parsley and cook, stirring often, for 10 minutes more. Set aside to cool slightly. Adjust the seasoning.

2. Meanwhile, preheat the oven to 400°F. Toss the eggplant in the remaining olive oil and season with salt and pepper. Lay the slices out in a single layer on a baking sheet and roast until tender, about 30 minutes. Set aside to cool.

3. To make the béchamel, melt the butter in a pot over medium-low heat, then add the flour, whisking constantly. Cook the roux for a couple of minutes, then add about 1 cup of the milk, whisking the sauce smooth until it thickens. Add a couple of more cups of milk; continuing to whisk and allowing the béchamel to thicken. Once all of the milk has been added, cook the sauce at a gentle bubble until it is quite thick, 10 to 15 minutes. Season with salt and pepper and set aside to cool. Whisk the béchamel occasionally to keep it smooth and to cool it faster.

4. Reduce the oven to 350°F. To assemble the moussaka, put all of the venison mixture in the bottom of a high-sided 9 by 12-inch baking pan. Layer the eggplant over the venison, overlapping if necessary and covering the entire surface. Add the egg yolks to the béchamel and whisk again to combine. Pour the béchamel over the top, making sure it is well covered. Sprinkle the cinnamon, nutmeg, and Parmesan over the top and bake in the oven until the custard is lightly browned, puffed, and cooked through, about 45 minutes.

5. Remove the moussaka from the oven and let it cool to room temperature so the béchamel sets. Once cooled, cut into large squares and serve with dressed summer vegetables. To serve hot, let the moussaka cool slightly so the béchamel sets. Then return to a 350-degree oven for another 15 minutes, until hot.

Venison Burgers

Adding in ground bacon and egg yolk keeps these burgers moist and adds lots of richness and flavor. Condiments for burgers are very relative to who's eating them, but a good, earthy cheese and mustard are prime additions for venison. Here, we recommend Emmentaler and coarse-ground mustard, along with some spicy arugula for texture. More bacon on top is not a bad idea.

1½ pounds ground venison

6 ounces bacon or pancetta, ground

Kosher salt and freshly ground black pepper

4 egg yolks

Dash (or more) Worcestershire sauce

1 tablespoon olive oil

4 slices Emmentaler cheese

4 good-quality hamburger buns, toasted
    or grilled

Coarse ground mustard

Mayonnaise (page 54)

Sliced dill pickles

A handful of arugula

Serves 4

1. Build a really hot fire in a grill or preheat a large cast-iron pan over high heat.

2. In a bowl, combine the venison, bacon, salt, pepper, egg yolks, and Worcestershire sauce, mixing well. Divide the meat into 4 balls and form 4 large, 1½-inch-thick patties.

3. Brush the grill or pan with a little oil and grill or sear the patties until very well browned on one side, about 5 minutes. Flip the burgers and add the cheese to the top. Cook about 3 minutes more for medium rare to medium. Serve on buns with mustard, mayonnaise, pickles, and arugula.

Sautéed Venison Liver

Venison liver is very strong, but quite good. When extremely fresh, the texture is almost indescribable—firm, dense, and rich. This recipe is at its very best the night that you've shot a deer, preferably at camp, accompanied by a great bottle of wine. We use an Indian spice mix called garam masala to season the liver, which tones down the iron flavor, adds a sweet note, and rounds out the bacon and pungent herbs. A little liver goes a long way. It's really good for you and shouldn't be missed, though this isn't the recipe that will convert liver haters (try the Goose Liver Pâté, page 131, for that). Serve with mashed potatoes.

8 to 12 slices of venison liver, about
  ½ inch thick

2 cups milk

8 slices high-quality bacon

2 onions, thinly sliced

1 small sprig rosemary, leaves only, chopped

Kosher salt and freshly ground black pepper

1 tablespoon garam masala

1 cup all-purpose flour

¼ cup **Venison Stock** (page 173),
  chicken stock, or water

2 tablespoons balsamic vinegar

¼ cup chopped fresh chives

Serves 4

1. In a bowl, soak the venison liver in the milk for an hour or two.

2. In a large sauté pan over medium heat, cook the bacon until crisp, about 10 minutes, and set aside. Drain and reserve the bacon fat, leaving about 2 teaspoons in the pan.

3. Add the onions to the pan and cook them slowly, stirring occasionally, until golden and tender, about 10 minutes. Add the rosemary and season with salt and pepper. Remove the onion-and-rosemary mixture from the pan and set aside.

4. Remove the liver from the milk and season with salt and pepper. In a bowl, combine the garam masala and flour and dredge the liver in the flour, shaking off the excess.

5. Add the reserved bacon fat to the pan and increase the heat to medium-high. Once the bacon fat is very hot, add the liver and sear each side until browned, about 1 minute per side.

6. Add the onion mixture back into the pan, along with the stock and vinegar, and toss gently to combine. Serve immediately, garnished with bacon and chopped chives, and with mashed potatoes on the side.

Grilled Venison Heart

I just happened to barely clip the heart of my last deer, leaving it auspiciously intact for this dish. The heart is possibly my favorite cut from the entire deer, because of its unique, firm texture and surprisingly mild, tenderloin-like flavor. I like to open the heart up, flattening it for grilling or frying, though you can trim as much of the sinew as you can without cutting into it, and then stuff it with herbs and bread crumbs for a dramatic presentation. Serve venison heart to someone you like a lot.

1 venison heart

2 tablespoons olive oil

1 teaspoon red wine or balsamic vinegar,
  plus more for dressing

2 garlic cloves, finely chopped

1 small sprig rosemary, finely chopped

1 small sprig parsley, finely chopped

1 small sprig thyme, finely chopped

Kosher salt and freshly ground black pepper

4 green onions

A handful of arugula

¼ cup pale green celery leaves

Serves 2

1. The day before grilling, clean and marinate the heart. Make a cut on one side of the heart and open it up like a book.

2. Remove any white sinew and all the stringy bits on the inside.

3. In a small bowl, combine the olive oil, vinegar, garlic, and herbs. Rub the marinade over the heart and refrigerate overnight.

4. Make a hot fire in a charcoal grill, or set a gas grill on high heat. Season the heart with salt and pepper.

5. Grill the heart until nicely charred and browned on both sides, but still pink inside, about 10 minutes total. Grill the green onions until lightly charred, 3 or 4 minutes.

6. Let the heart rest for 10 minutes, and then slice thinly. Serve with the grilled onions, arugula, celery leaves, and a few more drops of balsamic vinegar.

1

2

3

Butchering Turkeys

Being so much larger than other game birds, turkeys require a whole different approach when it comes to breaking them down. Pluck a turkey as you would any other bird, taking care not to rip the breast skin if you plan on roasting it whole. The copious breasts on turkeys lend themselves to quite a few different preparations, like cutlets (page 191) or sausage (substitute for venison, page 143 or substitute for goose, page 144), or terrines (substitute for dove, page 131). The livers can be used for pâté (page 132), while the gizzards and hearts can be used in confit (page 220). The well-exercised legs are tough and sinewy—and require very long cooking to become tender—but have wonderful flavor. The wings are very much worth plucking, though I only go to the first joint and cut there, leaving the wingtip and its stubborn feathers on. The wings have a good amount of meat on them, and can add a lot of flavor to stock, or can be slowly cooked in water and the meat shredded and used in potpie (page 192) and salpicon (page 174), served with dumplings (page 238), or braised (substitute wings for legs, page 194). While most turkeys are taken with shotguns and have relatively little damage done to the prized areas, some will be taken with rifles. Expect a good deal of trauma, and try to aim high, hitting the spine and leaving the legs and breast intact. Save the beautiful feathers as souvenirs.

Tools needed: a boning knife, and a meat mallet and plastic wrap if making cutlets

A. Wing
Brine, stew, or confit, or use in gumbo (page 216), or with pappardelle (page 232).

B. Breast, whole
Brine and smoke, grill, or roast.

C. Breast Cutlets
Panfry (Turkey Cutlets, page 191).

D. Leg Quarter
Braise or stew (Turkey Potpie, page 192, Tomato-Braised Turkey Leg, page 194), or substitute for Squirrel with Herb Dumplings (page 238).

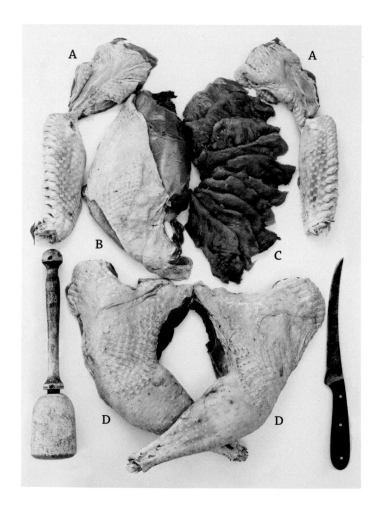

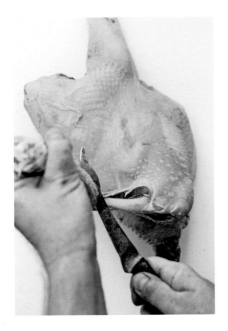

1 With the turkey lying on its side, make a cut along the wing bone to the first joint.

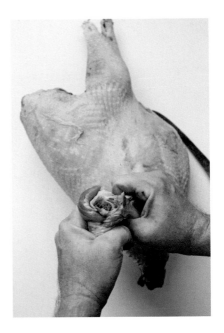

2 Grip the wing on either side of the joint with your hands and forcefully snap downward, breaking the joint.

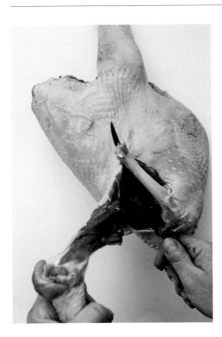

3 Cut back down along the wing bone to the breast, then cut away the large piece of meat found along the back. This yields a wing with two large pieces of boneless meat attached and is perfect for braising.

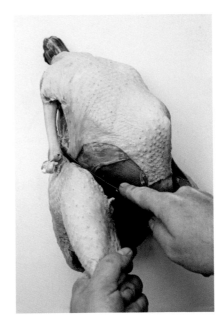

4 Make a diagonal cut between the breast and leg quarter, cutting all the way down to the spine.

5 Cut around the "oyster"—the round muscle just forward of the hip joint—with the tip of the knife.

6 Crack the leg downward, separating the leg quarter at the hip joint, and follow the spine to the tail, removing the leg quarter.

7 Repeat with the other leg.

8 Locate the breastbone running down the middle of the breast and cut down to the ribs just to the right of the breastbone, splitting the breast.

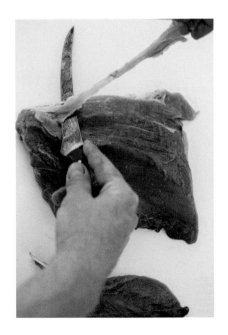

9 Follow the ribs with the knife and remove the first half. Repeat with the second half of the split breast.

10 For cutlets, remove the skin, silverskin, and sinew from the breast. Save this trim for turkey stock. Remove the tenderloin—the long, thin muscle at the base of the breast—and set aside for making into cutlets.

11 Slice the breast into pieces about ¾ inch thick.

12 Lay out one sheet of plastic wrap. Place the cutlets and tenderloin on top, and cover with another layer of wrap. Gently pound the cutlets to about a ¼-inch thickness.

Turkey Cutlets with Mushroom Gravy

Breaded cutlets are the gateway preparation for many dishes involving game meats. Pounded thin, breaded, and panfried, these tender bits of meats served with a rich sauce will win over anyone. This method is surely not limited to just turkey breasts, which we pound thinly (page 189), but is also great for venison or feral hog loin, or leg muscles, thinly sliced and pounded out. Even duck or goose breasts, skinned and flattened, would be perfect, especially with the game-friendly mushroom gravy.

By all means, feel free to use wild mushrooms, like morels, hen-of-the-woods, or chanterelles, which are especially good in this dish. Serve this with rice and slow-cooked greens.

2 eggs, beaten

1 cup milk

1 boneless, skinless wild turkey breast, about 1½ pounds, sliced thinly and pounded (page 189)

Kosher salt and freshly ground black pepper

2 cups plus 2 tablespoons all-purpose flour

2 cups fresh or store-bought bread crumbs

4 tablespoons unsalted butter

½ pound button, oyster, or crimini mushrooms, quartered

2 garlic cloves, chopped

2 cups Game Bird Stock (page 173), chicken stock, or water

2 cups heavy cream

Pinch of ground nutmeg

Juice of 1 lemon

½ cup olive oil

Serves 4

1. In a shallow bowl, whisk together the eggs and milk. Season each turkey breast cutlet with salt and pepper. Dredge each cutlet in the 2 cups of flour, then in the egg mixture, and then press gently into the bread crumbs. Set aside in the refrigerator.

2. Melt the butter in a saucepan over medium-high heat and add the mushrooms. Cook, stirring occasionally, until well browned, about 5 minutes. Add the garlic and cook for about 30 seconds, stirring. Add the 2 tablespoons flour and stir to combine.

3. Slowly add the stock, stirring constantly to avoid lumps, and bring to a simmer. Add the cream and nutmeg and simmer until thickened, about 5 minutes. Remove from the heat, add the lemon juice, and season with salt and pepper.

4. In a large sauté pan over medium-high heat, heat the olive oil until very hot. Add the cutlets, cooking in batches, without crowding the pan, and cook until golden, about 3 minutes per side. As they are done, transfer them to a tray lined with paper towels. Serve the cutlets with the gravy spooned over them.

Turkey Potpie

I adore potpies, probably because I grew up on a not-so-great version of them. Their silky texture, studded with meat, carrots, and peas, along with a crunchy, buttery, and even soggy crust, is true comfort. This recipe works well with any cut of game that needs long cooking, like duck legs, whole squirrels and rabbits, or even venison shanks and necks. I've even made potpies with fish, just adding some lighter vegetables, like fennel and parsnips; fresh herbs, like parsley and thyme; and a bit of lemon zest.

2 wild turkey leg quarters, or 8 wings

1 onion, halved

1 bay leaf

8 tablespoons (1 stick) unsalted butter

1 onion, chopped

4 medium carrots, thickly sliced

2 celery stalks, sliced

6 fresh sage leaves

¼ cup all-purpose flour

2 cups fresh or frozen sweet peas

4 small turnips, diced, their greens reserved and chopped

½ cup chopped fresh parsley

Kosher salt and freshly ground black pepper

One 12 by 12-inch piece of high-quality puff pastry

1 egg, to make an egg wash

Serves 8

1. In a large pot over medium heat, combine a gallon of cold water, the turkey legs, halved onion, and bay leaf, and bring to a simmer. Lower the heat and cook until tender, 3 to 4 hours.

2. Remove the turkey legs and allow to cool. Pull and shred the meat from the bones and refrigerate. Pour the broth through a fine-mesh strainer and reserve 3 cups for the potpie. Let cool and refrigerate the rest for another use.

3. Preheat the oven to 350°F.

4. In a 12-inch Dutch oven, melt the butter over medium heat. Add the onion, carrots, celery, and sage leaves and cook for 10 minutes, stirring occasionally. Add the flour and cook for another 2 minutes, stirring often.

5. Slowly add the reserved stock to the pot, stirring constantly to remove lumps. Bring to a bare simmer and turn off the heat. Stir in the peas, turnips, parsley, and shredded turkey and season well with salt and lots of black pepper.

6. Carefully cover the pot with the puff pastry, trimming the edges to fit and crimping the dough around the edge. Make a couple of ventilation holes with a sharp knife. Whisk the egg with a tablespoon of water and a pinch of salt; brush the pastry with the egg wash and bake the potpie until the crust is golden, about 45 minutes. Allow to cool slightly before serving.

Tomato-Braised Turkey Legs

Turkey legs are relatively large and muscular, and need long cooking to break them down. Braising in tomato sauce works for tough cuts because the acid cuts the fatty, sinewy rich-ness and breaks down the muscle structure, too. Substitute rabbit or squirrel, duck or goose legs, or feral hog shoulders.

2 wild turkey leg quarters, 3 to 4 pounds

Kosher salt and freshly ground black pepper

¼ cup olive oil

2 onions, chopped

4 medium carrots, thickly sliced

1 teaspoon dried sage

1 teaspoon fennel seed

1 cup red wine

Two 28-ounce cans crushed tomatoes

2 quarts Game Bird Stock (page 173),
    chicken stock, or water

Juice and zest of 1 lemon

¼ cup chopped fresh parsley

Serves 4 generously

1. Season the turkey legs well with salt and pepper.

2. Heat the olive oil in a large, heavy-bottomed pot over medium-high heat and brown the turkey legs well on the skin side only, about 10 minutes. Transfer the turkey legs to a plate.

3. Add the onions, carrots, sage, and fennel and cook, stirring often, until the vegetables are tender, about 10 minutes. Add the red wine and cook for another couple of minutes, and then add the tomatoes and stock. Bring to a simmer, return the turkey legs to the pot, and cover. Lower the heat and simmer until very tender, 4 to 5 hours, adding more liquid as needed to keep the turkey legs mostly submerged, and turning the legs periodically.

4. Season with salt and pepper and stir in the lemon juice and zest. Serve over Game Bird Polenta (recipe below) and top with the parsley.

Game Bird Polenta

1 quart Game Bird Stock (page 173)

2 cups heavy cream

1 bay leaf

1½ cups high-quality cornmeal for polenta

Kosher salt and freshly ground black pepper

½ cup grated Parmesan cheese

2 tablespoons unsalted butter

Serves 4

1. In a pot over low heat, combine the stock, cream, and bay leaf. Let the mixture warm for a few minutes.

2. Slowly add in the cornmeal, whisking constantly. Simmer until the polenta is cooked completely, 20 to 40 minutes, depending on the type of cornmeal. Stir very often with a wooden spoon to ensure that the polenta does not scorch on the bottom.

3. When done, remove the bay leaf, season with salt and pepper, and add the Parmesan and butter. Stir well and serve immediately.

Duck & Goose

DUCK : THE WELL-KEPT SECRET

We drive to the same pond where we hunted duck last year, and this time I'm not surprised when hundreds of Canada geese and ducks rise off the water as we approach with our shining flashlights and clanking decoys. This pond is a well-kept secret and hasn't been hunted all season. It's a gold mine.

About three dozen decoys are soon set, mostly pintails, in two clusters to the left and right of our grassy bank, in expectation of the birds landing into the wind between the

two groups. I'm on the left, Eliot's in the middle, and Jack takes the right. The birds are back immediately, with big flocks of teal circling above. It's impressive. The air is literally thick with birds, and when Eliot nonchalantly announces it's shooting time, it sounds like warfare. Before I know it, I've got two shovelers ("spoonies") and a green-winged teal down, all graciously fetched by Zorro. I'll never get over how nice it is to have a good dog along on a hunt. They seem to enjoy it even more than I do, and that's saying a lot.

Eliot is now vocally steering me away from the shovelers—whose aquatic diet can make them the least desirable of the puddle ducks for the table. (Though as

I write this, a pot of spoony-and-oyster gumbo is bubbling on the stove. It is indeed assertive, but also delicious, and served over rice from the very same prairie.) I start to pass on some shots in the increasing daylight for better chances at the tasty gadwalls that are now showing up in force.

Twenty minutes into legal shooting time, the action slows to a standstill and the high-flying geese take center stage. Last year, with a dense fog forcing low flights, Jack and I each scored a big specklebelly goose from low-flying flocks cruising over the pond. Remembering the way my big goose had thudded to the ground ten feet from my head then, I waste a lot of shots in a

vain attempt to down another one—the geese are flying too far up.

Groups of pintails and gadwalls are now working our spread of decoys, but aren't committing and are staying out of range. Maybe it's the bright sunlight reflecting off our gun barrels, maybe it's our unpainted faces or even Zorro's big black presence. Anyway, the shooting slows down and we pick off a couple of more birds here and there, including a suicidal green-winged hen that refuses to fly after landing in the decoys a mere ten yards in front of me. Eliot's goading and name-calling ("Hey, dumb bird!") finally annoys or frightens the bird enough to take flight, at which point I promptly harvest it. I do love to eat teal.

Finally, as the birds make it apparent that they are done for the morning and our hunger is setting in, we pack it up. Twelve birds among the three of us—plenty for the dinner we have planned for this evening, and some extra to take home to the family. With straps loaded with a mix of shoveler, teal, and

gadwall, and the auspicious addition of a delicious canvasback and a pretty drake redhead, we head into town to take the birds to the pickers (this tiny town has two businesses that pluck waterfowl) and grab some breakfast.

Hot coffee and some very spicy food are comforting, and we get a little rest before the evening's festivities. I busy myself making a mincemeat pie, onion and sage dressing, and glazed carrots while the others nap and a couple more guests arrive, including Jack's lovely wife, Anne, and Eliot's friend Sam, who we've been told can tell an exquisitely elaborate dirty joke.

The ducks are roasted rare with tangerines, just picked and supersweet. The snipe from the previous afternoon are wrapped in bacon and a sage leaf, then skewered shut with their own long beaks and roasted in a hot oven.

Toasts are made to the ducks, and Eliot insists that we face north to do it—it's a tradition, see. Sometimes it makes sense to have some ritual and formality; Eliot and Sam are dressed in black tie, and the ladies look great. There is a lot of bloody bird flesh on the table, and plenty of really nice French wine. Everyone is eating the birds with their fingers, which is pretty much the only way to eat a roasted duck after the first couple of knife-and-fork cuts.

Plucking Ducks

Ducks can be more difficult than other game birds because of their multiple tiny pinfeathers and stubborn down. These insulating feathers make for a longer and harder plucking experience, so just plan on spending a few more minutes with ducks and geese. I save the hearts, gizzards and livers from waterfowl, using the livers for Goose Liver Pâté (page 132) and the hearts and gizzards for Confit (page 220). I remove the wings completely from all ducks—there's just not any meat on them and they're really hard to pluck. I do the "mini spatchcock" on all birds except turkeys; this is the method that removes the backbone completely, which allows the bird to be cleaned easily, flattened (butterflied) for grilling, simply roasted, or stuffed.

Different ducks will warrant different preparations. Diving ducks, like ringnecks, scaup, and the like, can be strong-flavored and may be best skinned and used for something with a lot of spice, like Duck Tikka Masala (page 217) or Duck and Oyster Gumbo (page 216), where the musky flavor of these ducks actually shines. Northern shovelers (aka spoonies) fall into this category, too.

Puddle ducks, like gadwalls, wigeon, pintails, and mallards, are suitable for roasting (page 210), but will be excellent in the above preparations, or in Duck Yakitori (page 212). Redheads, though divers, can be excellent. Tiny, serving-size teal should be either roasted or grilled quickly, or long-cooked in a jar with fatty pork and herbs (page 215). Making a confit with the legs is an excellent idea, too; try making confit with teal or other small ducks split into halves.

Tools needed: a pair of sturdy shears

1 Hold the duck breast side up and the head away from you. Pluck the feathers from the breast, legs, and back by gently pulling them against the grain—slightly forward. This motion is like dealing cards.

2 Remove the wings by pulling them forward and cutting them with sturdy shears close to the breast. Try to not cut them at an angle, as this can make a sharp, bony point that will jab you.

3 Cut off the feet at the first joint and discard.

4 Cut off the head at the base of the neck.

5 Holding the duck breast side down, and with the neck facing you, cut along the backbone just to one side of it, almost to the tail.

6 Keep going, cutting out the vent and tail, just under the skin, all the way around to the other side of the spine.

7 Cut back along the other side of the backbone to the neck.

8 Pull the backbone down away from the neck, removing the entrails with it.

9 Remove the big gizzard. Now why throw this away? See page 23 for cleaning the gizzard.

10 Remove the liver if it hasn't been damaged by shot, taking extra care not to rupture the greenish gallbladder attached to the top. Carefully cut this away and set the liver aside.

11 Remove the little heart, which is tucked just under the breastbone. Remove the pinkish lungs from the interior of the rib cage and discard.

12 Rinse the duck well. A lot of the feathers will come out more easily when wet. If a lot of stubborn pinfeathers are still present, you can pass the duck over an open flame on the stove and singe them off.

Butchering a Duck or Goose

Ducks and geese are butchered identically. I usually remove the legs in quarters and take the breasts off the bone completely, at which point you can either leave the skin on or remove it for sausage (page 144) or Duck Tikka Masala (page 217). The carcass is then ready for being made into stock (page 173).

Tools needed: a boning or fillet knife

1 With the duck, breast side up, and the legs pointing towards you, make a diagonal cut between the breast and leg, pulling the leg away.

2 Continue to cut the leg away, following the bone. Make sure to get the little, round piece near the back—the "oyster"—using the tip of the knife.

3 Repeat with the other leg, removing the oyster.

4 Locate the breastbone running lengthwise between the breasts and make a cut on the right side.

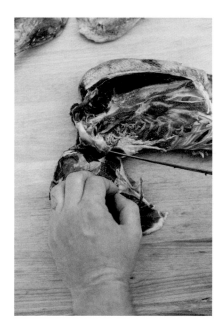

5 Cut to the bone, then, pulling the breast away, free the breast from the rib cage. Cut the breast from the carcass.

6 Repeat with the other breast, cutting down the left side of the breastbone.

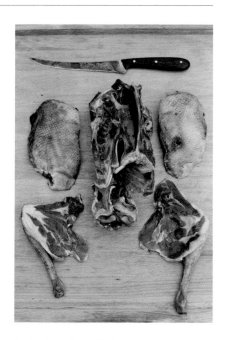

7 The broken down duck.

Roasted Duck with Tangerines

Roasting a duck whole seems like the respectful thing to do—after all, this bird flew all the way from Canada (maybe a few times) before you went and shot it. The red wine brine makes for a more flavorful, moist bird, accented by tart wine and spices, and tempers the assertive flavor of the duck. You will have to do some chewing no matter what—this is a primal preparation and will require picking up the duck and eating from the bones. Do not overcook a whole roasted duck, or it will be intolerably dry and have some of the livery iron flavor that game can have when overcooked. Choose mild-flavored puddle ducks like teal, gadwall, wigeon and mallards for roasting, and leave the diving ducks like ringnecks and bluebills for other preparations, like gumbo.

4 puddle ducks, plucked

1 gallon **Red Wine Brine** (page 211)

8 tablespoons (1 stick) unsalted butter, softened

Freshly ground black pepper

4 tangerines

4 tablespoons sugar

Serves 4 to 8

1. Brine the ducks in the red wine brine in the refrigerator for 12 hours. Remove the duck from the brine and dry very well with paper towels. Rub the breasts with the softened butter, and then season with pepper.

2. Preheat the oven to 450°F.

3. Cut the tangerines in half and sprinkle with the sugar. Place the duck and tangerine halves, cut side up, in one or two large cast-iron pans.

4. Roast the ducks to medium rare or medium (an internal temperature of 135° to 145°F), 10 to 20 minutes, depending on the size of the duck. Small ducks, like teal, should only take a few minutes, but the larger mallards will take longer. Baste the duck with the rendered fat every 10 minutes.

5. Remove the duck from the oven and let rest for a few minutes. Cut each duck in half down the breastbone, squeeze a roasted tangerine over the top, and serve.

Red Wine Brine

This flavorful brine adds a spectrum of flavors to duck, while playing off of its natural richness. Acidic wine tenderizes, the spices buff out the iron richness, and the sugar helps brown the birds during the roasting process. Use this brine also for pigeons and doves if you like: brine little birds for just a couple of hours.

One 750-ml bottle red wine

6 ounces kosher salt

½ cup packed brown sugar

1 tablespoon whole black peppercorns

1 cinnamon stick

2 whole cloves

Makes 1 gallon

1. In a pot, bring 3 quarts plus 1 cup water, wine, salt, sugar, and spices to a simmer. Stir well to dissolve the salt and sugar.

2. Let cool to room temperature and refrigerate. Once the brine is completely cold, it is ready to be used. Always discard a brine after use.

Onion and Sage Dressing

This simple dressing goes very well with large game and birds. Brown butter—butter which is cooked long enough to toast or brown the milk solids in the butter—adds a complex, nutty flavor to the sage and onions.

4 tablespoons plus 1 teaspoon unsalted butter

4 large onions, chopped

12 whole fresh sage leaves

Kosher salt and freshly ground black pepper

Pinch of ground nutmeg

8 cups of coarsely torn bread

3 cups Game Bird Stock (page 173),
    chicken stock

2 eggs, beaten

Serves 6

1. Preheat the oven to 350°F.

2. In a pot over medium-high heat, melt the 4 tablespoons of butter and cook until browned and nutty-tasting, about 2 minutes.

3. Add the onions and sage and season with salt, pepper, and nutmeg. Cook, stirring occasionally, until the onion is tender, about 8 minutes. Remove from heat.

4. In a large bowl, combine the torn bread, stock, and beaten eggs. Then add the onion and sage mixture, tossing well.

5. Grease a 9 by 12-inch baking dish with the remaining teaspoon of butter. Add the bread mixture to the baking dish and bake for 45 minutes, or until browned and bubbling. Serve immediately.

Duck Yakitori

The sticky, salty, and sweet sauce glazes and browns the duck, creating a nice exterior texture before the interior becomes overcooked. Try yakitori also with pieces of turkey breast or whole doves.

Pickled Radish (recipe below)

4 boneless duck breasts, about 1 to 1½ pounds

1 cup mirin (Japanese rice wine)

½ cup soy sauce

2 tablespoons sugar

2 tablespoons honey

3 garlic cloves, finely chopped

1 tablespoon oil

8 green onions, green part thinly sliced, white part cut into ½-inch pieces

8 bamboo skewers, soaked in water

Serves 4

1. Make the Pickled Radish 1 day prior to making the duck.

2. If the duck has skin, remove it with sharp knife and cut the duck into 1-inch cubes.

3. In a saucepan over high heat, boil the mirin, soy sauce, sugar, honey, and garlic until reduced by half, about 5 minutes. Remove from heat and set aside half of the sauce for serving.

4. Start a medium fire or preheat a grill. Toss the cubed breast meat in the oil. Thread the duck breast cubes, alternating with the white parts of the onions, onto 8 skewers.

5. Grill on one side for about 5 minutes, then turn, basting with the sauce. Continue grilling and basting until browned and the meat is firm but still a little pink inside, about 12 minutes total.

6. Discard any leftover basting sauce. Serve the duck with rice, green onions, pickled radishes, and the reserved sauce on the side.

Pickled Radish

Pickled radish goes well with grilled meats, especially those with a sweet glaze or sauce. Substitute cherry belle, watermelon, or French breakfast radishes.

1 medium daikon, peeled and thinly sliced

1 cup rice wine vinegar

1 cup sugar

1 tablespoon salt

Makes 1 pint

1. Place the daikon in a ceramic or glass bowl or jar. In a pot over high heat, bring 1 cup water, vinegar, sugar, and salt to a boil.

2. Pour the hot vinegar mixture over the daikon. Cover and refrigerate for at least 1 day. Serve cold. Pickled radish will keep well in the refrigerator for several months.

Teal in a Jar

This is an ideal recipe for a party. You can bake off these little ducks—sealed tightly in mason jars and slowly cooked with beans, bacon, sausage, and onions—and then reheat gently before serving. The cooking vessel also makes for a nice presentation. Quail, which are smaller, could also be used, but a teal just fits so nicely into a pint jar.

4 ounces dried cannellini or kidney beans, soaked overnight in water

4 whole teal, plucked and gutted

Kosher salt and freshly ground black pepper

12 ounces Venison Breakfast Sausage (page 140) **or other sausage**

4 ounces bacon, diced

2 onions, sliced

4 tablespoons sherry vinegar

2 teaspoons chopped fresh thyme

4 pint-size, wide-mouth Mason or canning jars

12 garlic cloves, peeled

2 to 3 cups Game Bird Stock (page 173), **chicken stock, or water**

Serves 4

1. Preheat the oven to 300°F.

2. In a small pot over medium-high heat, place the beans, cover with 4 inches of cold water, and bring to a boil. Boil for 20 minutes, then strain and reserve the beans, discarding the water.

3. Season the teal with salt and pepper. Remove the sausage meat from casings. Stuff each teal with one-fourth of the sausage and set aside.

4. In a small pan over medium heat, cook the bacon until it is crisp and rendered, about 10 minutes. Add the onions and cook for about 5 minutes, stirring occasionally. Add the vinegar and thyme, cook for 2 minutes, and set aside.

5. Place one-fourth of the onion mixture in each jar, followed by a stuffed teal. Add one-fourth of the beans and 3 garlic cloves to each jar. Ladle in as much stock as possible, leaving about a ½-inch space at the top. Place the lids on the jars and slightly tighten the screw bands.

6. Place the jars in a pan, add hot water to come halfway up the sides, and bake for 4 hours.

7. Carefully remove the jars from the oven. If serving later, cool unopened jars completely, then refrigerate up to 2 days. To reheat, place the jars in a pan and add hot water to come halfway up the sides. Simmer for 1 hour, or until the contents are bubbling.

8. To serve, let the hot jars cool slightly, and carefully open with a towel to hold the jar and lid. Serve from the jars or invert the teal into a bowl.

Duck and Oyster Gumbo

The rich flavor of wild ducks works perfectly with oysters in a gumbo, and if you have some less desirable ducks, such as shovelers or diving ducks, this is a great use for them. This recipe slowly cooks the roux in the oven—easier than a stovetop method—allowing the ducks to simmer while the flour and fat slowly brown and develop the characteristic nutty flavor of roux. Just stir the roux occasionally to ensure even cooking. If you can wait, refrigerate the gumbo for a day or two before eating; it develops more flavor that way.

3 wild ducks

1 cup lard or oil

2 cups all-purpose flour

1 pound Smoked Goose Sausage (page 144) or other smoked sausage, sliced

4 onions, chopped

1 cup chopped celery

1 cup chopped fresh parsley

1 tablespoon dried thyme

1 tablespoon dried oregano

6 dried bay leaves, ground

1 quart shucked oysters, with their liquor

Kosher salt and freshly ground black pepper

Cayenne pepper

Hot sauce

Thinly sliced green onions

Serves 10

1. Preheat the oven to 300°F.

2. Place the ducks with enough cold water to cover in a large pot. Bring to a simmer over high heat. Lower the heat, skim off any scum that rises to the top, and simmer the ducks until tender, about 3 hours.

3. Meanwhile, melt the lard in a cast-iron pan over medium heat and slowly stir in the flour to make a smooth paste. Place the pan in the oven and cook, stirring every 30 minutes or so, until the roux is a deep chocolate brown, about 3 hours.

4. When the ducks are ready, remove them from the pot and let cool. Pick the meat from the bones and refrigerate. Strain the stock, set aside 3 quarts for use, and cool and refrigerate the extra stock for another use.

5. While still hot, place the cooked roux in a heavy-bottomed pot over medium heat and add the smoked sausage, onions, celery, parsley, thyme, oregano, and bay. Cook, stirring often, until the vegetables are tender, about 10 minutes. Slowly add the reserved stock to the roux, stirring constantly, until it is absorbed and thickened. Cook for 2 hours over low heat.

6. Add the duck meat to the gumbo mixture and stir a few minutes to warm through. Turn off the heat.

7. Stir in the oysters and their liquor and let the oysters cook in the hot gumbo until they curl at the edges, about 5 minutes. Season with salt, black pepper, and cayenne. Serve with rice, hot sauce, and sliced green onions.

Duck Tikka Masala

Marinating duck in a spiced yogurt, then broiling it and simmering it in a heavily spiced tomato cream tames even stronger-flavored species, so this is a good use for a strap of ring-necks or shovelers. Please also try this traditional Indian recipe with wild turkey breast or even cubes of venison—the complex blend of spices works perfectly with most game.

Boneless, skinless breasts from 4 wild ducks, cut into 1-inch cubes, or 1 pound of cubed game meat

Kosher salt and freshly ground black pepper

1 tablespoon coconut oil or unsalted butter

1 onion, finely chopped

4 garlic cloves, finely chopped

One 1-inch piece fresh ginger, grated

1½ tablespoons garam masala

2 teaspoons cayenne pepper

One 28-ounce can crushed tomatoes

1 cup heavy cream

¼ cup fresh cilantro leaves

Marinade

1 teaspoon cumin seed

1 teaspoon coriander seed

1 cup plain yogurt

One 1-inch piece fresh ginger, grated

4 garlic cloves, finely chopped

½ teaspoon cayenne pepper or other chili powder

¼ teaspoon ground turmeric

Serves 4

1. To make the marinade, in a small skillet, toast the cumin and coriander seed over medium-high heat until fragrant, about 1 minute.

2. Combine all of the marinade ingredients in a glass or ceramic dish. Add the duck, season with salt and pepper, and toss well to coat. Refrigerate for 8 hours or overnight.

3. Heat the coconut oil in a stockpot over medium heat, and cook the onion, garlic, and ginger, stirring occasionally, until golden and fragrant, about 10 minutes.

4. Add the garam masala, cayenne, tomatoes, and cream. Lower the heat and simmer until slightly thickened, about 20 minutes.

5. While the sauce is cooking, preheat the broiler. Scrape the marinade from the duck and spread the meat out on a baking sheet. Broil the duck until browned, turning the pieces occasionally, about 10 minutes total.

6. Add the broiled duck pieces to the sauce and simmer for 10 minutes. Season with salt and pepper. Serve with steamed basmati rice and garnish with cilantro leaves.

GOOSE : OVER THE DECOYS

I'm lying on my back, staring at the silver sky streaked with cirrus clouds as a few geese swirl about, just out of range. Vicious prairie burrs sting every time I shift this way or that, and, despite this, I'm almost lured into sleep by the drone of thousands of roosting geese and the gentle coastal breeze.

Things could be worse. It could be cold and wet, which would make lying on one's back in a barely flooded marsh pretty uncomfortable. And there could be no geese at all, which is the reason I'm here in the first place. We have set up about four hundred white snow goose and a few dozen Canada goose decoys in the pre-dawn darkness. All the while a cacophonous drone emanates from the roosted swarm just to our north over the levee. As the legal shooting time approaches, one of our party sets forth to stir the giant flock into moving—hopefully, to get them up so that, eventually, they'll resettle in small groups amongst our decoys, at which time we will shoot them.

His movements along the other side of the dike of the northern rice field become obvious, as a tornado of agitated geese ascends in a cloud of cackles, easily two thousand strong. It is magnificent, and wakes me right up.

The swarm creeps to our left, then makes a move straight overhead. Crazy Andy forgets protocol and just shouts "Fuck it!" and four of us simultaneously do a crunching sit-up, point our shotguns straight in the air, and fire two or three rounds. All of the geese go eerily silent for a moment, then erupt in a chorus of honking consternation and betrayal. Immediately, they bank into the wind and flee with the thermals. This mass movement away from us is contrasted by three shapes plummeting to the ground, two straight down, one helicoptering in the tight circles of a wing-shot bird. Our first geese of the day thud to the earth heavily and with finality, as Chapman, a handsome black lab with devilish amber eyes and an erratic personality, races around, bringing them back to us. Three smallish but pretty specklebelly geese start a pile that will exceed two dozen by the end of the morning.

As the sun climbs higher and the geese begin to filter back in larger numbers, I try to put things into perspective. The back of my trigger finger is bloodied from the powerful recoil of the heavy goose shells. I've only slept about three hours, and I face a four-hour drive home, after I pluck all the geese. A single snow goose coasts directly into the decoys and Crazy Andy gives me the shot. It's a low, incoming shot—an easy one at thirty-five yards—and I sit up to take it. A black shape in my peripheral vision causes me to pause and pull the 12-gauge from my shoulder. Chapman has assumed that a goose landing so closely is a shot goose, and is racing toward it to pick it up. The goose, frightened by the black dog barreling down on him, flies up and over the decoy spread. With the dog out of danger, I fire and miss, twice. Randy suggests leading the big birds by about six more inches. Back on my back, I am thinking about a lot of things and how exactly I got to be here, staring at the clouds in some rural Texas field. There's danger, food, suffering, good dogs, money spent, and these huge birds that have traveled all the way from Canada. I'm going to make sausages out of these snow geese.

Confit

A popular tradition for a reason, confit means simply to cure lightly (or, in the past, heavily) in salt, then cook in pure fat. This process tenderizes, flavors, and preserves. If the items are left submerged completely in fat and kept cool, they can be stored for very long periods of time, as the fat creates an impenetrable barrier and thwarts spoilage, as does the salt. Our method employs less salt and is designed to be eaten sooner, but this confit will still keep refrigerated and stored under fat for a couple of weeks. Use very high-quality fat for this process—either nonhydrogenated pork lard or rendered duck fat. While this can be pricey, you can reuse the confit fat several times if you carefully remove the salty, gelatinous liquid that sinks to the bottom. Do not discard this stuff, though—even though it is salty, it is loaded with flavor and can be used to season a soup or sauce in small amounts. We prepare confits from just about anything, but duck and goose are typical and delicious.

1. Mix together the cure ingredients. Season the confit items with 1 tablespoon of cure per pound. Season all over with the cure, then lay all of the pieces in a nonreactive ceramic, plastic, or glass pan and refrigerate overnight.

2. The next day, rinse the pieces under cold running water and pat dry with paper towels. Place in a container—a ceramic crock or a large mason jar is aesthetically pleasing and functional—and cover the confit items completely with melted fat, making sure the items are totally submerged.

3. Bake, covered, in a 275°F oven, just so the fat gently bubbles. If it cooks too quickly or at too high a temperature, you will, in effect, fry the confit and it will be dry. Test for doneness after 2 hours. Some larger cuts will require 4 to 5 hours to become tender. Goose and duck legs will typically take 2 to 3 hours, as will the gizzards.

4. Once tender, carefully remove the items from the oven and let cool at room temperature in the fat; then refrigerate for at least a day or two, preferably 4 or 5.

5. To use, place the crock or jar in a warm oven or a pot of simmering water and reheat until the fat melts completely. Carefully remove the pieces you need then with clean tongs or a slotted spoon and drain them well, adding the drained fat back into the crock. Confit can be great simply grilled until browned and crisp, or used in dishes like Goose Leg Confit with Potatoes Sarladaise (page 222) or Salade de Gesiers (page 222).

Confit cure

8 ounces kosher salt

4 ounces brown sugar

6 sprigs thyme, coarsely chopped

4 bay leaves, torn

4 whole cloves, ground

Confit items

Duck or goose legs with thighs attached; duck or goose gizzards and hearts; small game, like rabbits and squirrels; whole small game birds, like dove, teal, and quail; pork ribs and pork chops

High-quality pork lard or rendered duck fat, as needed

Serves 4

Salade de Gesiers

I first had this salad in France at an unassuming little restaurant in a likewise unassuming little town. The rich gizzards, tart vinegar, and crisp lettuces were a revelation.

Large handful cleaned duck or goose gizzards and hearts (page 23)

1 onion, thinly sliced

1 small sprig thyme, chopped

2 tablespoons red wine vinegar

4 large handfuls fresh lettuces in peak condition

Kosher salt and freshly ground black pepper

4 thick slices of good bread, toasted with olive oil

Serves 4

1. Four or 5 days in advance, make a confit with the gizzards and hearts (page 220).

2. When ready to prepare the salad, rewarm the confit and drain well, reserving 1 tablespoon of the confit fat. Slice the gizzards and hearts and set aside.

3. Heat the reserved confit fat in a sauté pan over medium-high heat, add the onion and cook until tender and lightly browned, stirring occasionally, about 5 minutes. Add the thyme and sliced gizzards and hearts and cook for 1 minute more, then add the vinegar. Remove from the heat and let cool slightly.

4. In a large bowl, toss together the dressed confit and lettuces, and season with salt and pepper. Serve with the toasted bread.

Goose Leg Confit with Potatoes Sarladaise

These crusty potatoes are flavored with rich confit fat and enlivened by the addition of fresh, finely chopped parsley and raw garlic. The potatoes are stars in their own right and pair perfectly with confit. Add a large salad to compensate a little for the indulgence.

8 goose legs or 16 duck legs

2 pounds Yukon gold potatoes, sliced ½ inch thick

Kosher salt and freshly ground black pepper

4 garlic cloves, peeled

10 sprigs parsley, leaves removed

Serves 4

1. Four or 5 days in advance, make a confit with the legs (page 220).

2. When ready, rewarm the confit and drain well, reserving 2 tablespoons of the confit fat.

3. Preheat the oven to 400°F. Place the legs, skin side up, in one layer in a roasting pan. Place the pan on the top rack of the oven and crisp the legs for about 15 minutes.

4. Meanwhile, toss the potatoes in the reserved confit fat and season with salt and pepper. In a large, ovenproof pan over high heat, brown the potatoes on one side, about 5 minutes. Turn the potatoes and place the pan in the 400°F oven for 10 to 12 minutes, until browned on the other side and tender. Remove from the oven and allow to cool slightly.

5. Crush the garlic cloves with the flat blade of a knife and combine with the parsley on a cutting board. Chop the parsley and garlic together until very fine. Toss the herb and garlic paste with the potatoes and stir to coat well. Serve the confit over the potatoes with a side of salad greens.

Rabbit & Squirrel

RABBIT : ONE IS ENOUGH

The outlook was bad: no bunnies. This was a bit shocking, as Jeremy's modest ten-acre property had been loaded with the delicious little things for the previous two seasons. They had prospered among the old machinery, tall grass, brambles, and bushes on the farm, and on one outing last year, we shot four rabbits in ten minutes, then drank beer and cleaned them until dark.

But here we are, Jody and I, on this very crisp bluebird day, not quite ready to accept the disappointing news from Tink and Jeremy, who have patrolled the farm several times without a single rabbit sighting. Did the dogs get them? The coyotes? Is it some kind of natural population cycle? There are plenty of potential culprits.

The landscape has that late-winter quality; dead and dry, and it feels really good to walk around in it with a purpose, even if there are no rabbits. We tromp through the tunnels of ground-hugging vines, listening for the telltale rustling that precedes the bounding of an escaping cottontail, but see nothing except a few field mice, which are spared. We then hook to the south, to the field above the tiny almost-dry pond and its promising ravines, only to be disappointed again amongst the thick bankside weed stalks and deadfall limbs. A sweep back to the fence line through the dense piles of brush is hopeless as well. We cross the fence and go into the wild, untouched area laden with deep arroyo ditches and waist-high grass. Nothing. Not a single rabbit flushed or seen.

Back over the fence, feeling warmed in the sharp northern wind by all the activity, and carrying only a pocketful of 20-gauge shells, a game strap, and the side-by-side 20, we creep through fallen ragweed, through mesquite and open ground where the rabbits could be gathering to

fence in front of me. This is not innate reasoning; it's just the way they have always run in the past and a good place to start. He lifts the pallet and . . . nothing. We peer under the boards, seeing if a reluctant rabbit needs some prodding to make its escape, but there's nothing there except for a couple of field mice, which, again, we spare. The next pallet yields the same results, and the next. Finally, we lift a pallet and I am instantly firing my first barrel, then my second, before it even registers that I'm shooting at all. The first shot at the fleeing bunny misses; the next is placed in the line of the moving knee-high grass, right where the rabbit should be if I could still see him.

The grass stops moving. Jody and I look at each other. The stillness and quiet of the whole afternoon has been shattered so quickly and unexpectedly, it takes us a moment to regain our bearings. I walk over to where my last shot hit and gleefully find a fat, dead cottontail. A nice-size one, too, and judging by the dense pattern of the pellets, not badly hit, either. I declare this to be the happiest I've ever been about making a shot, and I'm telling the truth. Having been told that it couldn't happen does indeed make it sweeter. Jody snaps a picture and I cannot wait to show Tink that I found a bunny. We start cleaning the rabbit right away in the rapidly cooling evening.

There is something wonderful about cleaning warm game on a chilly, windy day. Feeling the flesh change from warm and living to cold, edible meat in your hands is an incredibly sincere way to experience the transition from life to death. It's especially at these moments that the game looks like good, delicious food to you even in its just-dead form; when guts and fur don't bother you at all and you can see the cooked rabbit in your mind. This one will likely end up stewed with cream and sweet wine, then tossed with pasta if I feel like picking through the meat, or maybe just fried and served with lemons. I quickly skin and gut the rabbit and we have an abbreviated sip of whiskey as the sun sets and it starts to get really, really cold.

feed before a very cold, clear night. But not today.

Our last-chance spot is around the old pens that once housed goats and a few turkeys but now have fallen into disrepair and therefore become an ideal rabbit habitat. The ground here is scattered with large pallets, old corrugated roofing, and the detritus of decades of farming. Under this, a colony of rabbits can thrive, mostly protected from hawks, owls, coyotes, and dogs.

The technique required here is different from the "flush and shoot" method used in the bushes. One of us must lift the fallen pallets, while the other, having positioned himself in the likely avenue of retreat, waits for the safe shot as the rabbit streaks out from under its upended home. We walk to the first pallet—a six by twelve-foot fallen roof from some long-defunct goat house—and pause. They have to be here. I face the fence, putting Jody behind me and to my side and wait while he lifts the heavy boards, ready for the rabbit to run straight for the

Cleaning Rabbits and Squirrels

I field dress rabbits and squirrels the same way, which I find to be easy. Jody tells me of East Texas techniques that are lightning fast, as these guys he hunts with out there shoot a lot of squirrels. I like this "sweater-and-pants" method.

Tools needed: a pocket knife or other thin-bladed, sharp knife

1. Cut off the squirrel's feet at the first (elbow/knee) joint. Remove the tail by breaking it forward, toward the head, and cutting through the vertebrae. Twist the head to break the spine, then cut off the head. Make a "waistline" cut, just through the skin, all the way around the squirrel, about halfway between the hind legs and forelegs.

2. Loosen the skin around the spine until you can get your index and middle fingers of each hand in there. Firmly grasp the skin and pull the "sweater and pants" apart.

3. Turn the skinned squirrel belly up with the shoulder end pointed toward you. With a sharp, thin-bladed knife, make a small incision right below the ribs, with the blade pointed upwards. Make a shallow cut from the rib to the pelvic bone between the back legs. Insert the knife tip under the pelvic bone, cut upward through the bone, and bend the legs apart slightly.

4. Cut in the opposite direction, through the ribs, all the way to the shoulders.

5. Hold the squirrel upright, grasp the entrails in the rib-cavity area, and gently pull down, removing all of the internal organs.

6. Wash the squirrel out well. Dry and then refrigerate.

1

2

3

Butchering Rabbits and Squirrels

I will generally cut rabbits and squirrels into 7 or 8 pieces for cooking: the back legs, front legs and 3 or 4 "saddle" cuts, which are basically cross sections of the remaining animal. These pieces are then ready for braising or frying.

Tools needed: a sturdy knife.

With the squirrel lying belly down, pull the back legs upward to separate them from the body at the joint. Cut around each hip and through the ball joint, removing the legs. Cut the shoulders from behind the shoulder blades where they meet the body. The shoulders will come right off. Cut through the body, perpendicular to the spine, by first cracking the spine at the vertebrae, then cutting through it with a sharp, heavy knife. Depending on size, cut this trunk piece, or saddle, into 3 or 4 sections.

4

5

6

Fried Rabbit

The rich flavoring of a brine, the tenderizing ability of acidic buttermilk, and the basic ease and appeal of frying makes this recipe perfect for small game animals. Feel free to vary the spices in the dredge, adding more hot pepper sauce, black pepper, or dried herbs. Serve with lemon wedges, mashed potatoes or potato salad, green beans cooked with garlic, and hot biscuits.

1 cup kosher salt, plus extra for seasoning

¼ cup sugar

6 bay leaves

2 lemons, halved

2 or 3 cottontails or 4 to 6 squirrels,
  cut into serving pieces (page 229)

2 cups buttermilk

A few drops of Tabasco or other hot pepper
  sauce

2 cups all-purpose flour

2 tablespoons freshly ground black pepper

2 teaspoons dried thyme

2 teaspoons dried oregano

2 teaspoons sweet paprika

1 teaspoon dried ground ginger

½ teaspoon celery seed

Lard or oil, for frying

Serves 4

1. In a large pot over high heat, combine the salt, sugar, bay leaves, and 1 gallon of water. Bring to a boil, dissolving the salt and sugar, and add the lemons. Remove from the heat and allow to cool; refrigerate until completely cold. Add the rabbit and refrigerate for 4 to 6 hours.

2. Remove the rabbit from the brine and toss with the buttermilk and hot sauce. Cover and refrigerate for a few hours or overnight.

3. In a large bowl, combine the flour, pepper, thyme, oregano, paprika, ginger, and celery seed and mix well. Remove the rabbit pieces and allow most of the buttermilk to drip off, then dredge well in the flour mixture. Lay the pieces out on a baking sheet and refrigerate until ready to fry.

4. Preheat the oven to 200°F and place a paper towel–lined pan on the oven rack.

5. In a large pot or Dutch oven, heat 3 inches of lard or oil over medium-high heat to 350°F. Carefully add the floured rabbit pieces to the pot and fry until deeply golden, 8 to 10 minutes, turning as needed. Do not crowd the pan. Cook in batches, if necessary, letting the oil return to 350°F between batches.

6. Remove the cooked pieces with a slotted spoon, draining the hot oil well, and transfer to the lined pan in the oven. Sprinkle each piece with a little salt as you go. Serve hot or at room temperature.

Rabbit in Pipian Sauce

This spicy, complex sauce really works well with most game, from venison and hogs to birds and squirrels. This version is not as complicated as many traditional recipes, but contains the basics: nuts, chiles, and spices. Pecans, being a very prolific in the region where I live (it's the state tree), create a rich base for the sauce, and are a fitting ingredient if you choose to make this with squirrel. Buy good dried chiles and Mexican cinnamon from a quality grocer, or Mexican market.

2 cottontails or 3 squirrels, cut into serving pieces

1 onion, skin on, halved

Kosher salt

1 cup pecans

3 dried chipotle chiles

5 dried ancho chiles

2 dried guajillo chiles

4 garlic cloves, unpeeled

1 teaspoon whole black peppercorns

1 small piece Mexican cinnamon (canela), about 1-inch long

¼ teaspoon cumin seed

1 tablespoon oil or lard

2 tablespoons apple cider vinegar

Serves 4

1. Place the rabbit, one onion half, and a pinch of salt in a pot. Cover with cold water and bring to a boil over medium heat. Lower the heat, and simmer until tender, 2 to 3 hours, depending on the age of the game.

2. Preheat the oven to 300°F. Remove the rabbit from the pot and set aside. Discard the onion and reserve 2 cups of the broth, saving any remaining broth for another use.

3. Spread the pecans on a baking sheet and toast in the oven until fragrant, 10 to 15 minutes. Remove from the oven and let cool. Once cool, process the pecans in a food processor until finely ground.

4. In a cast-iron pan over medium-high heat, toast the dried chiles for 1 minute on each side, then place them in a bowl and cover with 1 cup of warm water or some of the broth.

5. In the same pan over medium-high heat, add the unpeeled garlic cloves and the other onion half. Toast the garlic until the skins are browned and beginning to char. Char the onion until very black, about 20 minutes. Set the garlic and onion aside in a bowl.

6. In the same pan over medium-high heat, toast the peppercorns, cinnamon, and cumin until fragrant, about 1 minute. Remove the spices, let cool slightly, and grind in a spice grinder or mortar.

7. Peel the onion and garlic. Remove the chiles from the soaking liquid and reserve the liquid. Pull the stems and seeds from the chiles. Combine the pecans, onion, garlic, spices, chiles, and 2 teaspoons salt in a blender and add the soaking liquid from the chiles. Blend this to a smooth purée.

8. In a clean pot, heat the oil over high heat. Add the puréed sauce carefully to the oil and cook, stirring often, for about 10 minutes, adding some of the reserved broth, if necessary, to thin the sauce. Add the reserved rabbit and the vinegar and stir to coat. Serve with white rice, black beans, corn tortillas, and cilantro leaves.

Pappardelle with Rabbit, Muscat, and Cream

The blending of sweet flavors—muscat and fennel—with the rich flavors of wild rabbit and cream makes a balanced, savory pasta dish. By cooking the rabbit first in the sauce, then shredding the meat, you enrich the sauce and make eating small game easier. Doves could also be used in this preparation, but won't need to be cooked quite as long. We used pappardelle for this recipe, but any wide, flat pasta will work just fine. Substitute another sweet wine for the muscat, like Riesling or gewürztraminer.

1 cottontail or 2 squirrels, cut into braising portions (page 229)

Kosher salt and freshly ground black pepper

2 tablespoons olive oil or unsalted butter

1 fennel bulb, sliced

1 onion, sliced

2 cups thinly sliced green cabbage,

3 cups muscat or another sweet white wine

1 quart **Game Bird Stock** (page 173), chicken stock, or water

1 cup heavy cream

Zest of 1 lemon

¼ cup chopped fresh parsley

1 pound pappardelle or favorite flat pasta

Serves 4

1. Season the rabbit with salt and pepper.

2. Heat the oil in a large sauté pan over medium-high heat and lightly brown the rabbit on all sides, about 5 minutes total. Transfer to a plate.

3. Add the fennel and onion to the pan and cook until softened but not browned, about 10 minutes.

4. Add the cabbage, wine, rabbit, and enough stock to cover the rabbit by 4 inches. Bring to a simmer, lower the heat, and cook until tender, 1 to 2 hours, depending on the age of the rabbit. Add enough stock to the sauce to keep the rabbit submerged.

5. Once the rabbit is tender, remove from the sauce and let it cool slightly. Pick the meat from the rabbit and return it to the sauce; discard the bones.

6. Add the cream and continue to cook the sauce until slightly thickened, about 10 minutes. Stir in the lemon zest and parsley and season with salt and pepper. Keep the sauce warm over low heat.

7. Bring a large pot of water to a rapid boil and add enough salt to make it taste like seawater. Add the pasta and cook just until tender, 10 to 12 minutes. Drain very well in a colander. Add the cooked pasta to the warm sauce and toss to combine. Serve immediately on warm plates.

Squirrel : Three for Three

Squirrels have always appealed to Chris's East Texas core—Chris having grown up in the outer suburbs of Houston, precisely where, he'll have you know, *Urban Cowboy* was filmed. His Virginia-born grandfather instilled a tradition of squirrel cookery that hasn't faded in three generations, making it dangerous to be a squirrel living near the five-acre property Chris now inhabits, on the southern edge of the Blackland Prairie. Hunting at Chris's has always been a comfortable and genteel affair, because, between his small plot and the bordering hundred acres belonging to his friendly neighbor, we can hunt and be back at the house within minutes, cooking whatever we may have found. The neighbor's pond is small but loaded with big crappie and bluegills, and during the early fall, squadrons of blue-winged teal randomly swoop over. In the winter, doves will swarm this pond right before dark. It's a five-minute walk from the kitchen.

Today, we're looking for some squirrels. It's one of the first crisp days of fall, which arrives like a soothing gift after the inevitably hot summer, and Chris has graciously not hunted squirrels yet, so they might be a bit easier to find. Country squirrels are very, very wily, and can be difficult to hunt. The two-person approach is usually best, as a squirrel, once spotted, will usually hug the opposite side of the trunk, scooting out of vision. One hunter remains stationary while the second hunter simply moves around the tree and makes the shot. In theory. We use small shot-guns with full chokes that shoot tight patterns of pellets through the branches.

Today, we start hunting when we walk out the back door. The marauding squirrels in the area gorge themselves daily on Chris's chicken feed, which is annoying, but does make them fatter. We walk in a slow, wide loop beyond the cleared area dotted with oaks into the more scrubby, juniper-choked perimeter along the fence. He sees the tail first, flicking twice, framed against the gray sky about fifty yards away. I swing wide, aiming to come at the tree from the opposite direction while he slowly works his way directly toward the tree, shielded from my vision by its thick trunk. I finally am on the far side, stumbling over some matted greenbrier because I'm looking up, not down. I can't see the squirrel, but I'm sure it hasn't jumped to another tree. Then, there's a scooting movement as it skitter-hugs the post oak to the other side. Chris's 20-gauge booms and I see the squirrel fall and thud into the leaf pile at the base of the tree. Great. We need three more like this older male to make dumplings, but even just one more will do.

We climb over the fence to the neighbor's property and continue down the road to the creek, where massive overhanging pecans mingle with Mexican plums, making this a very good spot for squirrels. This is also away from our first shot, so hopefully, they won't be on alert and holding tight, or even worse, holed up in the hollows of the trees. I cross the creek, which is a stagnant trickle this time of year, and climb the steep bank on the other side. Now we can move in tandem down the creek, ostensibly flushing squirrels for each other to shoot. We go about a hundred yards when we hear the crackling of little claws on bark and see movement in a cedar elm on Chris's side of the creek. This squirrel is on the move, but at more of a concerned pace than a panic. Chris's shot drops the squirrel as it moves along a bare limb, and it conveniently falls

in a poison ivy–free spot twenty feet in front of him.

The next forty-five minutes are just a nice walk in the woods—the squirrels seem to have disappeared. Then, on the way back, more movement, and the unmistakable noise of a squirrel in a tree about thirty yards from the creek. We head toward the sounds, spread out to encircle the tree and move the squirrel. As we near the oak, it runs along a branch at the very top of the tree, then, inexplicably, it pauses, sits, and is promptly shot by Chris, who is now three for three.

Two of the squirrels are older males and will require some extra time in the pot to become tender, but it's worth it. If we head in now and get them cooking, they'll be ready just in time for dinner.

Squirrel Cooked over a Campfire

You can make this with minimal equipment and a few ingredients that keep well when camping or spending a day out. Just add squirrel. For quick, hot cooking like this, a smaller, younger, more tender squirrel is best, but if the squirrel you've got is older, it will do. There will simply be some more chewing involved.

3 or 4 slices of bacon, chopped

1 young, small squirrel, cut into pieces
(page 229)

1 onion, sliced

A few small potatoes, sliced

Kosher salt

Serves 1

1. Get the fire very hot. Build it up nicely with a lot of coals, and then add small- to medium-sized wood for instant heat. Get the pan very hot before adding anything, especially if it's cold outside.

2. Cook the bacon until it just starts to render fat. Add the onion, potatoes, and squirrel. Season well with salt.

3. Cook, stirring occasionally, allowing everything some time to sit in one spot and brown a bit. Flip and turn the potatoes and squirrel to expose them to the heat and bacon fat and allow them to crisp up nicely. Keep going until the squirrel is cooked through and the potatoes are done, 10 to 20 minutes total. Serve on a plate with some hot coffee.

Squirrel with Herb Dumplings

Slow-cooking game until it's tender not only yields falling-off-the-bone meats, but rich broths. These big dumplings are enlivened by fresh herbs and lemon zest, and don't have that heavy, dense feel of a traditional dumpling. You can also substitute duck, goose, or turkey legs for the squirrel in this recipe, with great effect.

2 whole squirrels or cottontails, gutted

1 onion, halved

4 whole cloves

1 bay leaf

8 tablespoons (1 stick) unsalted butter

6 medium carrots, thickly sliced

1 onion, diced

2 celery stalks, thickly sliced

¼ cup all-purpose flour

Kosher salt and freshly ground black pepper

Dumplings

2 cups all-purpose flour

1 tablespoon baking powder

½ teaspoon salt

1 tablespoon unsalted butter, cold

⅔ cup milk

1 egg, beaten

1 teaspoon chopped fresh sage

1 teaspoon chopped fresh thyme

1 teaspoon chopped fresh rosemary

1 teaspoon chopped fresh parsley

Zest of 1 lemon

Serves 4

1. In a large pot over high heat, combine the squirrels, onion, cloves, bay leaf, and 2 gallons of water. Bring to a simmer. Lower the heat, skim any foam that rises to the surface, and simmer the squirrels until tender, 3 to 4 hours, adding water, if necessary, to keep them submerged.

2. Strain the stock into another pot and discard the onion, cloves, and bay leaf. Reserve 2 quarts of stock and keep warm over low heat. Cool and refrigerate any leftover stock for another use. Allow the squirrels to cool slightly and shred the meat. Discard the bones and refrigerate the meat.

3. In a large heavy-bottomed pot or Dutch oven, heat the butter over medium heat until melted. Add the carrots, diced onions, and celery and cook until tender, about 10 minutes, stirring occasionally.

4. Add the flour and cook for 2 minutes more, stirring often. Add about 2 cups of the reserved stock to the pot and stir until thickened. Continue to slowly add the remaining warm stock. Keep the pot at the barest simmer—do not boil.

5. To make the dumplings, in a large bowl, stir together the flour, baking powder, and salt. Add the cold butter and pinch together with the flour until it is in small, pea-size pieces. Add the milk, egg, herbs, and lemon zest, and stir until just combined, gently and briefly kneading with your hands.

6. Add the shredded squirrel meat to the warm stock, and then drop golfball–size pieces of the dumpling mixture into the pot. Cover with a lid and let the mixture simmer for another 20 minutes, or until dumplings are fluffy and cooked through. Season with salt and lots of pepper. Serve hot.

The Spring Run

WHITE BASS : GO TO THE FISH

Our day starts early, with a one-hour drive north and east, through endless cornfields down the same roads we've traveled for years now. White bass—or "sandies" as they're known in North Texas for their preferred sandbar spawning sites—like to bite in the early morning, and will usually taper off a bit as the sun gets higher in the sky, especially on a clear day like this one. That means getting to the creek before sunup.

These little silver fish run up the muddy creeks of my home lake—a nondescript, turbid, and otherwise unlovable puddle on the prairie—in February and March, sometimes sooner, sometimes later. It seems to depend on the moon cycle, rainfall, and temperature. They love a rising creek beneath a full moon after a warm spring evening; the running water provides the oxygen their eggs need to survive, and these fish are here solely on a mission of procreation.

Many times I've made this hike and caught a white on my first cast. So anticipation is high this morning, and it's hard to walk slowly through the pre-dawn woods. The window to catch these fish is closing—the run may last another month, or maybe it's already slowing down—who knows? Some days we've caught nothing; others, I've sunk to my knees in the creek-side mud catching the twenty-five–fish limit without even moving from my first spot. Today seems promising, with its cold start and rapidly warming, still air, meaning low barometric pressure and, ostensibly, schools of ravenous white bass coursing upstream in a spawning frenzy.

Chris and I walk to the Bend, an elbow-shaped hard turn in the stream that has accumulated a hellishly prickly logjam with a series of deeper slow pools behind it. This is a great place to start, because it is the first narrowing of the stream from the lake, which the fish are leaving to find their way to the faster, clearer, and

shallower sandbars upstream. It's a natural bottleneck akin to an eight-lane highway closed down to one lane: Fish here.

Or so it seems. Today they're nowhere to be found, at least not en masse. I catch one legal white, then a tiny little male that sprays me with his milt as I release him, and hope that this is the worst thing that happens to me today. The strike of a white bass is an addictive thing; you slowly roll a tiny (the tiniest you can handle) jig (white or chartreuse) through slow backwaters and resting spots until it just stops with a short tug, like a flinch from a pulled punch. Then these little muscular fish fight. A twelve-inch fish on light tackle is not a done deal—whites pull with a primordial tenaciousness, planing hard in the current and heading for the nearest downed limb or cut bank. In the confines of a tiny steeply sloped creek, it can be tricky.

My one white bass looks lonely on the stringer as I struggle to find him company. Chris has since moved far upstream to wider and deeper waters, out of sight, and I wonder if he's having any better luck than I am. Over the years, we've developed two theories for catching whites. The first is the "Stay in the Spot" theory, where you catch a white and keep fishing that exact spot, making the same cast, over and over, until the next school comes by. It's boring but very effective. It also seems to be the technique of the older guys who fish out here, demonstrating how patience wins every time. The other is the "Go to the Fish" theory, where you walk upstream or downstream, hitting likely spots, catching the active fish and moving on. This is also effective, and better for those with short attention spans.

Today, I opt to find another spot upstream because I'm just not convinced the fish are here at the Bend. I move from the logjam to the small pool above, which is about twenty feet wide and sixty feet long. I cast the little horse-head jig with its wobbly spinning metal blade tight against the far bank and let it settle, then begin a

slow retrieve, a cadence that a young white-bass guide in East Texas taught me. Three casts into the pool and there's that lovely thump again. I've got a nice fish on. I pull it in and see it's a fat female, bulging with roe, which I think right away will be delicious fried in brown butter with lemon. She's strung and I keep casting. Nothing for about fifteen more minutes until my rod bows violently and a really big fish starts bullying me around the pool. A catfish, for sure. Big blues come up this creek with regularity, gorging on shad and crawfish, and conceivably white-bass eggs. Finally, I turn it just before it heads under the logjam to my right and see it's a big carp. Every spring, we catch a carp or two from these little creeks. This normally herbivorous fish sometimes takes on an aggressive streak and nails a jig, and it always surprises. The carp makes another screeching run and the line breaks. I've eaten carp before and liked it, but not out of a muddy little stream like this, so it's not a huge loss, aside from the jig.

I fish for another few minutes, and nothing. Moving downstream, I spot exactly what I'm looking for— another bottleneck just a hundred yards up from the Bend, and this time I can see the fish.

Whites are so determined to make it upstream that sometimes they'll skim across shallow bars, salmonlike, just to make it to the next hole. I see a white skidding up a sandbar and look for my avenue of approach. The banks of this creek are ridiculously steep, slippery, and covered in poison ivy. Most of the creek is inaccessible because of the ten- to fifteen-foot drop down to the water, but this spot has the slightest switchback trail, which will allow me a backhanded downstream cast to the pool below, where the whites are waiting and resting for a few seconds before they hurdle rocks and logs to reach the next pool. I slowly and carefully make my way down the mud-slick bank and settle my boots into sturdy tree roots. To my left, a small logjam sits at the top of a quick-moving chute of water that tapers, fanlike, into a dark pool to my right. A huge sagging branch hangs right over the pool, blocking any cast to its deep heart. I can, however, make a cast to the far bank and allow my jig to wash in the current down into the pool, and this technique pays off on the first cast. Bam! Another fat female goes on the stringer. This is the spot; I found them. I call for Chris, but he's surely out of earshot. An hour passes and the whites come with regularity, about once every ten minutes or so, each time with the same surprising strike. One slams into my jig just as I'm about to lift it from the water, and circles and splashes right below me until I tire it out and carefully swing it onto the bank beside me. Chris walks by and I give up my position to him and move downstream, precariously, to another spot that's so steep I'm leaning against the bank. A couple more fish are added to the stringer, and Chris is getting into them now, too.

Eventually it's time to go to work, and when I start to leave, I slide right into the water, swamping my knee-high boots in the freezing creek. This isn't the first time I've been dunked in these waters, and likely not the last. Twice, while wading here by myself, I've taken a step and never felt bottom— just the icy-cold water hitting my face and pouring down my waders. It's a terrifying sensation. Each time, I was close to the bank and grabbed the omnipresent roots to hoist myself back to stable footing. I do love white bass—they're the very first fish of the season—running up the creeks when it's still technically winter and bitter cold, but I don't wade alone for them anymore.

The walk out seems shorter than the walk in. We've got a nice little stringer of whites that we will cook with some of our canned tomatoes, garlic, olives, and capers. On the way back to the truck we pass only one other person who is willing to make the trek in, and he has fish, too.

Filleting Panfish

This method is very efficient for smaller fish, or when you've got a lot of them. The top-down style negates having to gut the fish, you just cut the fillet off of the bones all the way to the belly, then take the skin right off. I fillet almost all of my fish this way—white bass, crappie, sunfish in freshwater, and whiting, speckled trout, and croaker in salt. If you want to save the bones for stock, then take the guts and gills out after filleting and give the bones a good rinse.

Tools needed: a fillet knife

1. With the knife angled forward toward the eyes, make a cut on one side of the fish right behind the gill, as deep as the backbone from top to bottom.

2. Using the tip of the fillet knife, cut along the backbone starting at the head.

3. Cut down until the rib cage ends, then, keeping the knife flush against the backbone, cut through the bottom half of the fillet and through the skin near the anus.

4. Holding the knife against the bones, continue to cut down to the tail, cutting through the skin.

5. Come back to the rib cage and lift the fillet up with your non-knife hand. Using the tip of the knife, cut through the first series of bones on the rib cage, pulling the fillet away as you do. As the fillet is freed, run the knife along the rib cage all the way to the bottom of the belly, then through the skin. Repeat on the other side.

6. Now you have the fillets, skin on. Skin side down, remove the flesh by running the knife at a slight angle against the skin, and holding the skin at the tail end between your thumb and forefinger.

If you've caught a panfish full of roe—like a plump female white bass—remove the roe for cooking.

1. Before filleting the fish, make a cut from the anus to the pectoral fins between the gills with a sharp knife, pointing the blade upward and using only the very tip. Be very careful to cut just through the skin.

2. Open the incision and remove the two egg sacs with your fingers, gently cutting them free.

3. Soak them in ice water for a few minutes, then dry well and refrigerate until ready to cook.

1

2

3

4

5

6

Remove the roe before filleting

1

2

3

White Bass Roe in Brown Butter

When the fat white-bass females look like foot-balls, you know you've got some delicious roe to go with the fillets. Carefully remove the roe before filleting (page 248), and cook as soon as possible. The roe tastes much like the fillet, with a firmer texture that can be a little grainy if overcooked, so take care to sauté the eggs quickly over high heat. The combination of brown butter—nutty, toasted butter—garlic, parsley, and lemon is a traditional preparation for skate wings and sweetbreads (thymus glands), and works beautifully here.

Roe sets from 4 white bass or other fish

Kosher salt and freshly ground black pepper

2 cups all-purpose flour

8 tablespoons(1 stick) unsalted butter

4 garlic cloves, finely chopped

¼ cup chopped fresh parsley

Juice of 2 large lemons

Serves 4

1. Season the roe with salt and pepper, then dredge in the flour, shaking off the excess.

2. Melt the butter in a heavy-bottomed sauté pan over medium-high heat. Allow the butter to cook for another minute or two, watching closely until it turns a light shade of brown. When small bubbles forms and the butter foams slightly and smells pleasantly nutty, increase the heat to high. Add the roe sets to the pan and cook for about 1 minute per side. Once cooked, transfer the roe to warm plates.

3. Turn the heat down to medium and add the garlic and parsley to the butter. Let them sizzle for a few seconds, then remove the pan from the heat and stir in the lemon juice. Spoon the butter sauce over the roe and serve immediately.

White Bass Escabèche

Basically pickled fish, escabèche is a vibrant and delicious way to serve stronger-flavored fare. I particularly love dense, white bass fillets for this, though many of the non-delicate saltwater species, like mackerel, cobia, or amberjack work well, too. The citrus zest is an integral part of this recipe, as is the hot jalapeño. I like this served as an appetizer in the hotter months, with beer.

4 medium white bass fillets, about 1¼ pounds

Kosher salt and freshly ground black pepper

¼ cup olive oil

4 garlic cloves, thinly sliced

Zest of 1 orange removed in large strips
    with a peeler

Zest of 1 lemon removed in large strips
    with a peeler

1 red onion, thinly sliced

2 jalapeño peppers, thinly sliced

1 red or yellow bell pepper, thinly sliced

1 teaspoon dried oregano

1 teaspoon dried thyme

4 sprigs fresh thyme

4 bay leaves

1 cup white wine vinegar

1 cup white wine

Serves 4 to 6

1. Season the fillets with salt and pepper.

2. Heat a large sauté pan over medium-high heat and add the olive oil. When the oil is hot, sear each side of the fish, about 3 minutes per side. Transfer the fillets to a glass or ceramic container where they will fit in one snug layer.

3. Lower the heat to medium, add garlic to the pan, and cook for about 30 seconds, taking care not to burn it. Scatter the orange and lemon zest over the fish and add the garlic on top.

4. In a pot, bring the remaining ingredients and ½ cup water to a boil. Pour the brine over the fish and allow to cool to room temperature. Cover and refrigerate overnight. Serve cold.

White Bass Veracruzana

This Mexican sauce with Spanish influence adds fresh flavors to any fish. I like fish that have been breaded and panfried, as here, but grilled or baked fillets work well too.

2 tablespoons plus ½ cup olive oil

1 onion, thinly sliced

1 red or yellow bell pepper, thinly sliced

4 garlic cloves, thinly sliced

1 teaspoon dried oregano

Kosher salt and freshly ground black pepper

2 cups crushed tomatoes

¼ cup pitted green olives

4 tablespoons capers, drained

4 medium white bass fillets, about 1¼ pounds

2 cups all-purpose flour

1 egg

½ cup milk

1 cup fine bread crumbs

¼ cup chopped fresh cilantro

Serves 4

1. In a saucepan, heat the 2 tablespoons of olive oil over medium heat. Add the onion, bell pepper, garlic, oregano, and a pinch of salt, and cook, stirring occasionally, until the onion is tender, about 10 minutes.

2. Add the tomatoes, olives, and capers, and simmer over low heat for about 20 minutes.

3. Season the fillets with salt and pepper.

4. Mix together the egg and milk. Dredge the fillets in the flour, shaking off excess. Dip in the egg wash and then in the bread crumbs, coating well.

5. In a large heavy-bottomed pan over medium-high heat, heat the remaining ½ cup olive oil. When the oil is hot, carefully put the fillets in the pan and cook until golden on each side, about 4 minutes.

6. Transfer to a rack or paper towels. Serve the fillets immediately over rice, with the sauce on top, and sprinkled with the cilantro. Serve with Sautéed Zucchini (recipe below).

Sautéed Zucchini

This is my favorite way to enjoy good summer squash. Choose firm, small zucchini or yellow squash, as they'll have fewer seeds and a better texture. Serve with grilled or fried fish.

3 tablespoons olive oil

1 pound zucchini, cores removed, cut into ½-inch pieces

1 large onion, chopped

4 garlic cloves, minced

Kosher salt and freshly ground black pepper

Serves 4

1. Heat a sauté pan over high heat until very hot.

2. Add the olive oil, zucchini, and onion and stir a couple times. Let it sit undisturbed in the pan to brown, about 1 minute. Stir as necessary and continue to brown without allowing anything to burn. Cook until the squash has caramelized nicely and the onions are fragrant, about 10 minutes total.

3. Remove the pan from the heat, add the garlic, and toss to combine. Season with salt and plenty of black pepper, and serve.

CRAPPIE
THE NIGHT BITE

Hitting the crappie right at their spawn, their most vulnerable time for a bank-bound fisherman, is a mix of meteorological and folkloric postulating. Some adhere to the full moon (I do not, favoring the new moon instead), some go when the dogwoods (or redbuds) bloom, some when the bluebonnets come in, and some when the barometer is dropping below twenty-nine and not before.

These fine eating, gregarious fish nose into the shallows of murky lakes, nesting in tangles of brush so dense that you can sometimes walk on them. Here, a tiny jig dangled in front of them will elicit a thumping strike, followed by a short, brutal fight that simply involves slinging the catch with a modicum of finesse onto the bank before it spits the jig. It is fast, full-contact, and hypnotic fishing, punctuated by the thump and the attempted broadside escape of a flashing crappie.

Or, you can go at night and bring them to you. Lanterns, with their warm light and soothing low propane hiss, lowered just above the water, start a chain of events that betters your odds with these mercurial, schooling fish. The lanterns attract insects, which then attract minnows, the preferred forage of the huge-mouthed crappie, a fish that engulfs its prey by flaring its gills and sucking it in. That's the thump.

We are walking to the creek from our campsite this evening with this thump in mind. Everybody is equally rigged, carrying long rods, buckets of live minnows, buckets to hold the gear (and then invert for a seat),

floats, hooks, and lanterns. Extra propane bottles if you're smart. Beer if you're smarter.

We set up on a likely bank—one that has a deep undercut and proximity to deeper water, where the fish will hold during the hot day, ranging to shallower water at night, drawn by the yellow halos of light. Setup is quick, I bait one rod while I get the others ready. I fish two rods, Mark fishes three, Chris fishes two, and my dad fishes one, because he is one of those people who really doesn't care if he catches a fish. To his credit, he buys an equal share of minnows, a respectable quality in a fishing partner.

My minnow is deployed and I rig a white jig on the other rod, my preferred method. Mark has three minnows out already and is watching intently. You can get "Bobber Head" easily on these nights, a

disorienting feeling and headache brought on by watching neon plastic floats on a dark background for too many hours without respite. Occasionally, it pays to have a look around the creek, giving the eyes a rest and taking in the underrated beauty of these Blackland Prairie waterways with their high muddy banks and myriad oaks, bois d'arcs, and wild plums and pecans, all woven with greenbrier. Squirrels dart about in the waning light, and beavers often swim by. We always try to talk calmly when the beavers pass, hoping not to startle them into a fish-scaring tail slap. The vicious, squealing feral hog fights and the owl hoots will come later, long after dark.

It's wholly unnecessary to have the minnows out this early, as the action won't happen until it's just getting dark. We have a half hour until then, and we begin to settle in. Schooling crappie often run by size, and the first fish, usually small, always come right at the cusp of the evening. Our bobbers start to dip under quickly or steadily disappear in the muddy water, an effect that's almost hallucinatory, as your depth perception can be off and your bobber just seems to fade away. Sometimes the stick bobber pops, then lies flat, signaling an "up bite," where the crappie has grabbed the minnow and continued upward, creating slack in the line and causing the bobber to just fall flat. It took us a couple of seasons to figure this one out, but when we did, it was revelatory. The big ones tend to bite this way.

Mark catches a plump little green sunfish and I convince him to try for a catfish using it as bait. For some reason, these sunfish specifically are preferred by catfish. They look like fat, tiny bass with traces of

orange. He has an extra heavy rod and rigs the sunfish on it, then flings it to the other side of the creek and forgets about it.

The crappie come at their typical pace, which is in a flurry. With several minnows in the water at any given time, the bites happen as schools cruise through. One bobber dips, one disappears in a strong strike, and one just starts moving off to the side. Mayhem ensues. I miss the first fish, tangling the rig in the branch above me, and the second fish I hook by grabbing the rod with my other hand and getting lucky. I drop the first tangled rod and carefully swing the fat crappie toward the bank, as Mark does the same with a matching fish. That's two in the basket. Twenty minutes pass and nothing, not a bite. Then, a bobber tips over and sits still, petulant, before slowly and steadily moving toward the far bank. Another fish. A minute later, another, and another. A tiny crappie, scarcely six inches long, attacks a minnow and is caught,

to my chagrin. Bait stealer. At some point in the night, Mark's sunfish starts moving away at a rapid rate. He virtually dives for the rod before it is pulled into the creek and fights a six-pound blue cat to the bank. A bonus.

This continues into the night with one, two, or even three crappie being tossed into the wire basket suspended over the creek channel with an old rope. By midnight, we are straining to pull the basket from the water to add fish, as it's loaded with about three dozen fat crappie, vibrant in their spawning black-and-whites. I wrap the rope around an arm-size branch and carry it out that way.

Keep crappie alive as long as possible, and then get them on ice quickly. Though they have some of the best tasting fillets of any freshwater fish, they tend to get soft, especially in warm climates like where I live. Their fine texture and delicate flavor are perfect for frying, or making into croquettes.

Crappie Croquettes

Use almost any kind of fish for these simple cro-quettes. Snapper, drum, and whiting from salt water are great, and any freshwater fish will work, too. Serve the croquettes as a first course with different sauces for some variety.

1 tablespoon olive oil

1 onion, sliced

Kosher salt and freshly ground black pepper

One 28-ounce can crushed tomatoes

¼ cup chopped fresh basil, cilantro, or parsley

1 pound potatoes, such as Yukon golds
   or russets, peeled and quartered

1 pound crappie or sunfish fillets

Zest of 2 lemons

Pinch of ground nutmeg

2 eggs, beaten

3 cups unseasoned bread crumbs

Olive oil or lard for frying

Herb Mayonnaise (page 54)

Aïoli (page 76)

Lemon wedges

Serves 8 as a first course

1. Heat the olive oil in a large saucepan over medium heat. Add the onion and cook, stirring occasionally, until tender, about 5 minutes; add a pinch of salt. Add the tomatoes and simmer for 1 hour over low heat, until thickened. Remove from the heat, add the chopped herbs, and season with salt.

2. Place the potatoes in a large pot with enough cold water to cover. Season generously with salt and bring to a simmer. Cook until tender, 10 to 15 minutes.

3. Add the fish fillets and cook for 3 to 4 minutes until tender.

4. Drain the potatoes and fish and put in a large bowl. Season with salt and pepper; add the lemon zest, nutmeg, eggs, and ½ cup of the bread crumbs. Mash all of this together until homogenous.

5. Form walnut-size balls of potato-fish mixture and flatten them to make fat cakes. Set aside.

6. Heat a large heavy-bottomed pan over medium-high heat and add oil or lard to a depth of ½ inch.

7. Press each cake into the remaining bread crumbs to coat, and fry them until golden brown, about 2 minutes per side. Drain on paper towels or wire racks.

8. Serve the croquettes immediately with the tomato sauce, herb mayonnaise, aïoli, and lemon wedges.

Gratin of Crappie and Potatoes

In Spain, you'll encounter potatoes cooked with fish—usually salt cod—in myriad presentations. This is a simple riff on that: potatoes, fish, and cream. I like this as its own main course, but it is equally good paired with another, more simple, fish presentation, like a whole grilled fish.

1 pound potatoes, very thinly sliced

2 tablespoons unsalted butter, softened

Kosher salt and freshly ground black pepper

8 ounces crappie fillets, thinly sliced

Pinch of ground nutmeg

1 teaspoon chopped fresh thyme or
 ½ teaspoon dried thyme

2 cups heavy cream

Zest of 1 lemon

Serves 4

1. Soak the potatoes in cold water for at least an hour or overnight, then drain well.

2. Preheat the oven to 375°F.

3. Butter the bottom of an ovenproof baking or gratin dish, then add one layer of sliced potatoes. Season with salt and pepper.

4. Add a layer of fish, followed by a layer of potatoes, then another layer of fish. Continue, ending with a layer of potatoes.

5. Whisk together the nutmeg, thyme, cream, and lemon zest, then pour over the potatoes and fish. Cover tightly with aluminum foil and bake for 45 minutes.

6. Remove the foil and bake for another 45 minutes, or until browned and bubbling. Serve immediately.

Index

Suggested Reading

Aidell, Bruce and Denis Kelly. *Bruce Aidell's Complete Sausage Book.* Berkeley, CA: Ten Speed Press, 2000.

Andries de Groot, Roy. *The Auberge of the Flowering Hearth.* New York, NY: Ecco Press, 1996.

Barlow, John. *Everything but the Squeal.* New York, NY: Farrar, Straus and Giroux, 2008.

Bertolli, Paul. *Cooking by Hand.* New York, NY: Clarkson Potter, 2003.

Camp, Raymond R. *Game Cookery in America and Europe.* New York, NY: HP Books, 1990.

David, Elizabeth. *Elizabeth David Classics.* London, UK: Grub Street, 1999.

Don, Monty and Sarah. *From the Garden to the Table: Growing, Cooking, and Eating Your Own Food.* Guilford, CT: The Lyon Press, 2003.

Fallon, Sally. *Nourishing Traditions: The Cookbook that Challenges Politically Correct Nutrition and the Dieting Dictocrats.* Warsaw, IN: New Trends Publishing, 1999.

Farr, Ryan. *Whole Beast Butchery.* San Francisco, CA: Chronicle Books, 2011.

Fearnley-Whittingstall, Hugh. *The River Cottage Cookbook.* Berkeley, CA: Ten Speed Press, 2008.

Fearnley-Whittingstall, Hugh. *The River Cottage Meat Book.* Berkeley, CA: Ten Speed Press, 2007.

Gray, Patience. *Honey From a Weed: Fasting and Feasting in Tuscany.* New York, NY: Harper & Row, 1987.

Grigson, Jane. *Charcuterie and French Pork Cookery.* London, UK: Grub Street, 2008.

Guggiana, Marissa. *Primal Cuts: Cooking with America's Best Butchers.* New York, NY: Welcome Books, 2012.

Guste, Roy F. *Gulf Coast Fish: A Cookbook.* New York, NY: W. W. Norton and Company, 1997.

Henderson, Fergus. *The Whole Beast: Nose to Tail Eating.* New York, NY: Ecco Press, 2004.

Innes, Jocasta. *Your Country Kitchen.* Charlotte, VT: Garden Way Publishing Company, 1982.

Kaminsky, Peter. *Pig Perfect: Encounters with Remarkable Swine and Some Great Ways to Cook Them.* New York, NY: Hyperion, 2005.

Kowalski, John. *The Art of Charcuterie.* New York, NY: Wiley, 2011.

McGee, Harold. *On Food and Cooking.* New York, NY: Scribner, 1993.

McLagan, Jennifer. *Fat: An Appreciation of a Misunderstood Ingredient, with Recipes.* Berkeley, CA: Ten Speed Press, 2008.

Mettler, John J. *Basic Butchering of Livestock and Game.* North Adams, MA: Storey Publishing LLC, 1986.

Meyers, Perla. *The Seasonal Kitchen: A Return to Fresh Food.* New York, NY: Fireside, 1989.

NAMP. *The Meat Buyer's Guide: Meat, Lamb, Veal, Pork and Poultry.* New York, NY: Wiley, 2007.

Reynaud, Stéphane. *Pork and Sons.* New York, NY: Phaidon Press, 2006

Ruhlman, Michael and Brian Polcyn. *Charcuterie: The Craft of Salting, Smoking, and Curing.* New York, NY: W. W. Norton and Company, 2005.

Schneller, Thomas. *Kitchen Pro Series: Guide to Meat Identification, Fabrication and Utilization.* Independence, KY: Cengage Learning, 2009.

Shaw, Hank. *Hunt, Gather, Cook.* Emmaus, PA: Rodale, 2011.

Waters, Alice. *Chez Panisse Menu Cookbook.* New York, NY: Random House, 1995.

Acknowledgments

Completing this book has taken us all over the state, and it is a big state. To the many people who have contributed in so many ways, we offer our most sincere thanks.

Tamara, thank you for letting me go "to work", a thinly veiled request to go fishing and hunting, while you took care of our beautiful daughter, Paloma.

Without the incredible Dai Due staff that worked extra hours and made sure everything was going well in my many extended absences, thank you. To Tabatha Stephens, our most loyal, die-hard and wonderful leader, thank you. Thanks also to Kara Chadbourne, Greg Baldwin and Deepa Shridhar for keeping the shop open and being so damn cheerful. To my friend and colleague Morgan Angelone; none of this would be possible without your incredible work ethic, patience, organization (Morganization), cooking skill and humor.

To our friends David Clements and Cynthia Englund, who lent their beautiful kitchen to us for days on end, letting us shoot their squirrels, catch their catfish, ransack their wine cellar, burn their firewood, drink their espresso, and scare their ducks, thanks. Loncito Cartwright has been a constant friend, an example of good living and an instigator of great times fishing and hunting all over South Texas; it is always a pleasure to be around you and your family. Martin and Heather Kohout have been advocates, editors, dinner companions, and inspirations to us; their ranch is a model property, their children are amazing, and their pranks are well executed and clever. To Eliot Tucker, who knows how to hunt ducks the right way—with class—and how to spend the evening after a hunt in style.

Thanks also to my father, Dan Griffiths, for taking me fishing when I was little, taking me fishing a couple of weeks ago, and every single trip in between. Thanks to my mother, Sam Elkins, for the constant support and love, and George and Betsy, for incubating a distinct love of travel and spotting animals at great distances.

To my Grandma Daisy, who is a water moccasin shooting, squirrel-hunting, big trout-catching, whisky-drinking, chicken-fried steak–eating badass. I hope my daughter grows to be like you; gregarious, sweet, and slightly dangerous.

To my fishing buddy of many years, Christopher Martin, thanks for the countless trips to the coast, the river, and that trashy lake that you hate so much but go to anyway. Flounder fishing, eating oysters and watching westerns in coastal shacks represent some of my fondest memories *ever*. With patience and luck, you might even someday catch as many fish as I do.

To Mark Marsee, the crappie-obsessed, anarchist carpenter, thanks for the endless hours of drowning minnows and stalking the banks of muddy creeks in search of the thump.

Thanks also to Tink, Margaret Salzer, Martha Hopkins, Scott and Brenda Mitchell at Montesino Ranch, Jack and Ann Sanders, Kara Kroeger, Carol Ann and Larry at Boggy Creek Farm, David Burk, Adam Levine, Todd Duplechan and Jessica Maher, Mike Ortiz, Brad Wolfe, Ramona Liszt, Kate LeSueur, Sean Johnson, Sam Crocker, Eliza's Close to The Beach House in Port A, Josh Randolph, Jeremy Nobles, and Robert Selement.

To the guides: Captain David Dupnik, Butch Findley, Crazy Andy and J.J. Kent, thanks for putting us on the spots.

Jody would like to acknowledge his wife Regan for her patience and support while he was in the field. And also his grandfather, Joseph Palmer Moore, whom he describes as "the greatest sportsman I have ever known."

— *J.G. & J.H.*

Afield: A Chef's Guide to Preparing and Cooking Wild Fish and Game
Jesse Griffiths   Photographs by Jody Horton

Published in 2012 by Welcome Books®
An imprint of Welcome Enterprises, Inc.
6 West 18th Street, New York, NY, 10011
(212) 989-3200; fax (212) 989-3205
www.welcomebooks.com

Publisher: Lena Tabori
President: H. Clark Wakabayashi
Editors: Alice Wong and Katrina Fried
Designer: Gregory Wakabayashi
Food Stylist: Johanna Lowe
Editorial Assistant: Delisa O'Brien

Library of Congress Cataloging-in-Publication Data on file

ISBN: 978-1-59962-114-2

First Edition
10 9 8 7 6 5 4 3

PRINTED IN CHINA THROUGH ASIA PACIFIC OFFSET INC.

If you notice an error, please check the website where there will hopefully be a posted correction. If not, please alert us by emailing info@welcomebooks.com and we will post a correction.

Please note that in areas where Chronic Wasting Disease is present, there may be some risk in using or cutting venison bones and spinal tissue. Check with your local DNR for information and current warnings about CWD.

For further information about this book please visit online:
www.welcomebooks.com/afield

For further information about the author and photographer please visit online:
www.daidueaustin.net   **www.jodyhorton.com**